THE ENGLISH LANGUAGE DEBATE

One Nation, One Language?

—Multicultural Issues—

Paul Lang

ENSLOW PUBLISHERS, INC.

44 Fadem Road   P.O. Box 38

Box 699   Aldershot

Springfield, N.J. 07081   Hants GU12 6BP

U.S.A.   U.K.

Library of Congress Cataloging-in-Publication Data

Lang, Paul (Paul C.)
    The English Language Debate: One Nation, One Language? / Paul Lang.
        p. cm. — (Multicultural Issues)
    Includes bibliographical references and index.
    ISBN 0-89490-642-9
    1. Language policy—United States—Juvenile literature.
    2. English language—Political aspects—United States—
    Juvenile literature. 3. English-only movement—United States—
    Juvenile literature. 4. Education, Bilingual—United States—
    Juvenile literature. [1. English-only movement. 2. English
    language—Political aspects. 3. Education, Bilingual.] 1. Title. II. Series.
    P119.32U6E55 1995
    306.4'4973—dc20   94-31225
                                                                      CIP
                                                                       AC

Printed in the United States of America

10 9 8 7 6 5 4 3 2

Photo Credits: American Cancer Society, p. 48; Anonymous, p. 22; Archive of
Folk Culture/American Folklife Center/Library of Congress, pp. 58, 66; Brown
Brothers, p. 35; Kevin Cruff/Children's Television Workshop, Big Bird © 1994
Jim Henson Productions Inc., p. 84; Martin Simon, p. 91; National Park Service
Collection/Statue of Liberty National Monument, p. 37; Pieter Bruegel, 16th
Century painting, p. 17; Yuhong Zheng, pp. 64, 80.

Cover Illustration: Enslow Publishers, Inc.

Contents

Acknowledgments

I would like to thank the following people for their assistance and encouragement in helping me complete work on this book:

David Carle, aide to Senator Paul Simon of Illinois; Mark Magner, Prints Manager at the Children's Television Workshop; Gerald Parsons of the Archives of Folk Culture, American Folklife Center, Library of Congress; The Research Department staffs at the Boston and Brookline Public Libraries; Karen Rouse, vice president for Marketing and Communications at the American Cancer Society, Massachusetts Division; Yuhong Zheng and Jade Ang.

Special thanks to Mindy Hirschfeld and the editorial team at Enslow Publishers and to my family for their interest and support.

One Nation, One Language

In the United States, most people don't even think about the fact that they are speaking English until either they run into someone who speaks a foreign language or they travel abroad. After all, the songs on the radio, billboards on the highway, newspapers, school textbooks, job applications, and street signs are nearly all in English in this country.

A Fight Over Words

So it sometimes comes as a surprise when people born in this country meet a tourist or a recent arrival to the United States who can't understand what they say. They may try repeating words very slowly or very loudly, as though the other person's difficulty was a learning disability or deafness. Eventually they may even get impatient and angry, wondering what this person who can't even speak English—the language of the land—is doing in America.

The foreign tourist or immigrant in the United States, on the other hand, may be doing some wondering of his or her own. Why do so few people born in this country speak more than a couple of words of any language but English? And why do so many Americans seem annoyed that anyone in this country, even as a visitor, can't speak and understand English?

This situation of two or more people who can't understand each other because they speak different languages is at the heart of a political and social cause called the "Official English" or "U.S. English" movement. Supporters of this movement believe that government and schools should do everything they can to get all Americans to use English at school, at work, and in other public places. Opponents believe that while English is important, other languages have their place in the United States too, and that lawmakers and teachers should encourage recent arrivals to America to keep their native language while they learn English. In addition, opponents also believe that people born here should study the language and cultures of other countries.

Since the early 1980s, supporters and opponents of the Official English movement have made their arguments passionately—in the Congress, in the courts, in school board meetings, and elsewhere. Each side has felt misunderstood and unfairly treated by the other, and this controversy over words has sometimes become an angry fight, complete with ugly name-calling on both sides of the issue.

We can understand some of the issues involved in the movement by looking at the background, achievements, and opinions of Joe Bernal and Linda Chavez, who are both Hispanic Americans—citizens whose parents or more distant ancestors spoke Spanish. The vast majority of Hispanic Americans speak and understand English. In fact, there are as many Hispanic Americans who speak no Spanish at all as there are those who speak little or no English.[1] Still, the Hispanic-American population contains the largest single group of people in this country whose native language is something other than English.[2]

The following stories of Joe Bernal and Linda Chavez demonstrate how differently two Hispanic Americans view the issue of bilingual education, that is, teaching a student English while at the same time providing education in his or her native language. The controversy over English in the United States may be only a fight over words, but as these stories show, the emotions raised on both sides of the issue are very real.

Joe Bernal, Champion of Bilingual Education

By any standards, Joe Bernal is a Hispanic-American success story. He grew up on the West Side of San Antonio, Texas, was elected student council leader of his high school, became a teacher himself, served as a Texas State Senator, and is now a school administrator in San Antonio. Beginning in the mid-1960s, Senator Bernal worked to pass laws allowing students in Texas who did not have English as their native language to receive bilingual education.

At the high school he attended in San Antonio in the

7

1940s, 99 percent of the students were Mexican Americans, like Bernal himself. However, the school had strict rules about students speaking Spanish. Students were required to wear ribbons saying "I Am an American—I Speak English" and faced detention or even beatings if they were heard speaking Spanish to each other. One of Bernal's duties as student council leader was to turn in others he heard disobeying the rule.

When Bernal started teaching during the 1950s, he carried out a policy of fining his students a penny each time they slipped and forgot to speak English. The money went toward class parties at holidays. The policy was popular with the parents of his Hispanic students, who wanted their children to learn English as quickly as possible. "I used to collect a lot of money from these kids," he recalls.[3]

By the 1960s, when Bernal entered the Texas legislature, he had come to believe that laws against bilingual education had been put in place not to help foreign-born students but rather to keep them in their place. He was successful in overturning a state law that actually made teachers criminals if they taught any classes (except those specifically set up to teach foreign tongues) in languages other than English. Finally, in 1969, Texas lawmakers repealed the state law and teachers could no longer be fined or forced to give up their teaching licenses if they explained a word or concept in Spanish, or another language, in the classroom.

In May of 1969, Bernal wrote an essay called "I Am Mexican-American" in which he explains how his change of heart came about and he began to understand what effect enforcing speaking only English had on Hispanic students. He describes a Texas high school where 98 percent of the students were Mexican American. There, a student named Ector asked his classmate for a pencil. He spoke in Spanish. Ector, who was born in the United States and whose brother was fighting for America in Vietnam at the time, was immediately sent to the vice-principal's office.

There, he received a fifteen-minute lecture on why Americans are supposed to speak English and was made to repeat the rules about not speaking Spanish at school. Ector was given the choice of getting three "licks" (paddlings) or having one of his parents come to school to hear about his misbehavior. Since Ector's mother did not speak English, if one of his parents was to come, his father would have to take off from work, and end up with a smaller paycheck at the end of the week. Ector, who had not been paddled by his father since he was eight, took the whipping.

Although the school district had changed its policy by the time he wrote his article, Senator Bernal had become convinced by this time that the policy of speaking only English that he himself had enforced as a high school council leader and as a teacher was holding Spanish-speaking students back. By overturning the anti-bilingual teaching law, he could take pride in helping to make it possible for Mexican-American students to take a number of Spanish-language courses, like sociology and chemistry, "formerly considered too difficult for 'Mexican' children."[4] These types of classes were necessary if the high schoolers wanted to attend college.

Bernal has suggested that when a student starts speaking Spanish to a classmate, the teacher should not snap, "You're American. Speak English." Rather the teacher should "say something like 'Yes, Spanish is a great language—even Thomas Jefferson said so. You need English, though, to live and work in the United States.'"[5]

Linda Chavez, Defender of English— "The Tie That Binds"

Linda Chavez grew up in a poor neighborhood of Denver, Colorado, during the 1940s and 1950s, the daughter of an Irish-American mother and a Spanish-American father. While in high school, she took part in protest marches against segregation (separating people by race). She taught Chicano (Mexican-American) literature while a graduate student in the early 1970s and went on to edit and write articles for over six years for *American Educator*, a respected magazine for teachers. In 1985, she became the highest-ranking woman in Ronald Reagan's administration, directing the President's efforts to encourage public and congressional support for his policies. Since the late 1980s she has written and spoken out in favor of the English language. She sees it both as the tie that binds our country together and as the key to success for new arrivals to America.

Chavez has criticized bilingual teaching and other school programs that encourage students who don't have English as their cultural native language to maintain their native language and culture. This means spending more time teaching them to read and write English better. "Hispanics who learn English will be able to [take advantage] of opportunities....Those who do not will be [confined] to second-class citizenship. I don't want to see that happen to my people," Chavez wrote in 1988 while president of U.S. English, an organization fighting to make English the official American language.[6]

Chavez talks in this quotation about what's best for "my people," but both her background and her views are not typical of recent Hispanic arrivals to this country. Some Hispanics have wondered if she really had their best interests at heart when she fought against bilingualism and accepted the presidency of the U.S. English organization in 1987. The family of Chavez's Spanish-American father could trace their American roots back more than three hundred years, and according to James Crawford, author of *Hold Your Tongue: Bilingualism and the Politics of "English Only,"* Chavez, who "spoke no Spanish herself...lecture[d] others on the evils of bilingualism" and was seen by many in Denver's Hispanic community, where she grew up, "...as a traitor who had sold her [Spanish] surname to anti-Hispanic causes."[7]

In 1988, after fourteen months as president of U.S. English, Chavez resigned her post when a memo from 1986 written by the organization's founder, John Tanton, first became public. In shocking and sometimes vulgar terms, Tanton portrayed Hispanics as people who were flocking to immigrate legally and illegally to this country and overwhelming native citizens. He argued that these people were too stupid to educate, uninterested in public affairs, a people who were used to giving and taking bribes as part of their "tradition." He argued, wrongly, that Hispanic Americans never use contraceptives and could eventually outnumber other Americans who did. In a particularly tasteless and hurtful passage, Tanton wrote, "Perhaps this is the first instance in which those with their pants up are going to get caught by those with their pants down."[8]

Chavez has explained that she had never seen the "secret" memo before it appeared in a newspaper story and had never heard John Tanton discuss these kinds of opinions before. In a 1988 interview with James Crawford, she said that she resigned as president of U.S. English as soon as she finally came face to face with the Tanton memo and the anti-Catholic and anti-Hispanic prejudices it contained, which she found disgusting and "not excusable."[9]

But it may be too easy to dismiss Linda Chavez's views because of her embarrassing experiences with U.S. English. In her 1991 book *Out of the Barrio*, she argues that bilingual education often separates Spanish-speaking students from their classmates for several hours during the day and may actually keep them from being able to succeed in advanced classes where the English used is more difficult. Spanish-speaking students may also be at a disadvantage when they go after their first job if they have been kept "...outside the mainstream of this society—speaking their own language [and] living in protected" areas where they don't have to learn English.[10]

As a teenager, Chavez never felt encouraged by her teachers to do well in school or to prepare for college.[11] In *Out of the Barrio* and elsewhere, she has argued that Hispanic Americans can reach "the American dream" by aiming as high as they can, learning English as a way of getting ahead, and not using language as an excuse for living separate lives from other Americans.

"I'm very proud of my heritage," Chavez told a newspaper interviewer in the 1980s, "I've never run away from being Hispanic." But, she goes on, that doesn't mean she has to support blindly the "Hispanic" point of view. As Chavez sees it, she has carried on the traditional views of her conservative father who taught her as a girl that "...You have to think about things, decide what's wrong and do something about it and that's that."[12]

What is at Stake in the English-Language Controversy?

The English-language movement has focused attention on a problem that has been around ever since the United States became an independent country. The two sides of the problem can be put this way:

- As Joe Bernal believes, Americans who don't speak English as their native language should be encouraged to keep their own language while learning English. English speakers, on the other hand, should learn foreign languages.

- Following Linda Chavez's argument, schools and law-makers should encourage Americans with other native languages to learn and use English as quickly as possible. They should not be encouraged to maintain their native language. By adjusting to society at large and the majority language, these citizens will be able to achieve success in the classroom and the workplace.

In the chapters ahead, we will explore why the controversy has become so heated in recent years and how recent immigrants, especially teenagers and other young people, have coped with problems of language, cultural heritage, and adjustment to American society. We will also see how even students who have only spoken English their whole lives have a lot at stake in this debate, as they learn (or don't learn) foreign languages and as they decide for themselves what place other languages should have in the United States.

The Battle
Over English

Look at any American coin minted in the last 120 years and you will find words in a foreign language: "E PLURIBUS UNUM," a Latin phrase meaning "OUT OF MANY, ONE." The idea behind this national motto is that the United States is made up of different states and all kinds of people, but all have united into a single nation and share a common outlook and common values.

Why We Need One Language

It is an ancient idea that people speaking different languages will not be able to live together in harmony. In fact, *Genesis*, the first book of the Bible, tells the story of an early time when all people spoke the same language, lived together, and cooperated with each other. According to the Bible, when these people tried to build the Tower of Babel all the way to heaven, God punished them by making each person unable to understand the speech of every other person: we still speak of a "babel" of voices when many people are talking without understanding each other. Once the workers on the Tower of Babel lost the ability to communicate, they were unable to continue working together and were scattered over the face of the earth.

Supporters of the Official English movement believe that people of the United States must have a common language so that "out of many, one" united nation can grow strong instead of breaking up into dozens or hundreds of different groups, each with its own language and culture. "It is with a common language that we have dissolved distrust and fear," among different groups in American society, argues S.I. Hayakawa, author, educator, Republican U.S. senator from California from 1977 to 1983, and a strong supporter of the U.S. English movement. And he continues, "It is with language that we have drawn up the understandings and agreements...that make a society possible....[We must have] one official language and one only, so that we can unite as a nation."[1]

Both Senator Hayakawa and a Democratic senator from Kentucky, Walter Huddleston, have opposed the way bilingual education programs expanded in the 1970s and 1980s and have proposed that we add an amendment to the Constitution of the United States making English the official language of the land. Among other things, such an amendment would require that schools concentrate on making sure that their graduates had a command of English and studied all their subjects in English from an early grade. Some supporters of an

According to the first book of the Old Testament, Genesis, God punished mankind for building the Tower of Babel and trying to reach heaven, by making people speak different langauages. Pieter Bruegel painted his vision of the Tower in 1563.

"Official English Amendment," like Richard Lamm and Gary Imhoff, the authors of *The Immigration Time Bomb*, point out that "school dropout rates for students with limited English ability are lower when bilingual programs are used."[2] Critics of the U.S. English movement believe that these dropout statistics are reason enough to maintain ambitious bilingual education programs. But Lamm and Imhoff argue that it is unreasonable to expect government to make sure that every possible student graduates. "If we can't afford school dropouts," they write, "...then we can't afford immigration."[3]

Senator Huddleston, who served as United States senator from 1973 to 1985, maintained that an Official English Amendment is necessary not just to maintain the unity of the nation but to help protect recent immigrants from the "unfortunate" consequences of programs like bilingual education that had originally been created to help them make their way into American society. According to Huddleston, bilingual education, set up as a transition into full-time instruction in English, often continues for years and keeps its students "in a state of prolonged confusion, suspended between two worlds" where the subtle message is "that the mastery of English is not so important, after all."[4]

The supporters of the U.S. English movement have not only concentrated on trying to pass the Official English Amendment to the Constitution and to limit bilingual education. They have also worked for changes in the special services the government provides to non-English speakers, and they want to enforce the speaking of English in the everyday conversations of Hispanic Americans and others when they express themselves around native English speakers. For instance:

- In 1980, almost 60 percent of the voters in Dade County, Florida (which includes the city of Miami), approved an anti-bilingual ordinance. As a result, "Fire safety information pamphlets in Spanish are prohibited, Spanish marriage ceremonies are halted, and public transportation signs in Spanish are removed."[5] In 1983, the U.S. English organization did help to amend the ordinance, to provide emergency services, tourism and trade, and services essential to the aged and handicapped, in their own language.

- Nearly two-thirds of San Francisco voters approved a measure in 1983 to call for a change in federal law so that "the City and County of San Francisco need print ballots, voters' handbooks, and other official voting material only in English."[6]

- Thomas G. Dunn, the mayor of Elizabeth, New Jersey, issued a memo in 1983 instructing city employees that "English is the primary language to be spoken in the official conduct of city business." He went on to observe that "it is most discourteous for city employees to converse in other than English in front of other city employees."[7] The memo would, for instance, discourage friends at work from chatting in a common language if an English-speaker was present, even on break or lunch in the cafeteria. A United States district judge in 1990 struck down an Arizona law as a violation of free speech because, like Mayor Dunn's memo, it restricted government employees from using any language but English on the job.

The views of the U.S. English movement have found support among many Americans. An estimated *three out of four* English-speaking Americans support the idea of making English the official language of the United States, according to polling and voting results. However, 74 percent of language minorities also support official English.[8] Between 1981 and 1990, fifteen states adopted measures making English their official language, sometimes by huge margins in public referendums: 73 to 27 percent in California and 84 to 16 percent in Florida, both states with large numbers of people whose first language is not English.[9]

In the last chapter, the example of Linda Chavez, who spoke proudly of her father's Spanish heritage but opposed bilingual education, showed that even some Hispanics worry that speaking Spanish will keep them out of the mainstream of American society. When the citizens of Dade County, Florida, passed the 1980 anti-bilingual ordinance mentioned earlier, seven in ten non-Hispanic whites voted in favor as did almost half of the African Americans, but one in seven Hispanics voted for it, too.[10] A Spanish-speaking mother in a Dallas, Texas, *barrio* (Hispanic-American neighborhood) told an interviewer that she didn't want her children's school teaching them in Spanish since, as she explained, "It's because our people don't speak good English that holds us back. You know it's true—even a Spanish accent can hurt a person in life."[11]

Richard Rodriguez, a Mexican-American author, has also criticized the idea that Hispanic ethnic pride should keep children from learning English from the very start of their education. In his 1982 memoir *Hunger of Memory: The Education of Richard Rodriguez,* he tells how difficult it was for him to enter an English-speaking classroom knowing only a handful of English words and admits that he wouldn't have been so afraid that first day if teachers had spoken to him in Spanish. "I would have trusted them and responded with ease," he writes. However, he adds, "But I would have delayed...having to learn the language of public society." Rodriguez believes it is "a tragedy and a luxury" that Spanish speakers can live their whole life in America without learning English.[12]

Language as a Tool and as a Weapon

Richard Rodriguez sees English as a necessary tool that new arrivals to the United States need in order to succeed in public situations: the classroom, the workplace, and in their dealings with institutions like government and the courts. He has harsh words for the defenders of the Official English movement, however.

Rodriguez is upset by the hostile, frightening language the Official English supporters have used towards recently-arrived

Many people, like Richard Rodgriguez, are frustrated by the hostile, frightening language and tactics the Official English supporters have used towards recently arrived immigrants. These Chinese Americans dressed up in patriotic costumes are at a rally in New York City to sell government bonds around 1917.

immigrants. He argues for flexibility not only from the new arrivals to America, but also by native English speakers. "We must remind the immigrant that there is an America already here," he writes. "But we must never forget that we are an immigrant country, open to change. If we lose our public generosity, we will protect our language, certainly, but we will have lost our reason."[13]

It is this "public generosity" that seems in short supply when the issue is immigration and immigrant languages. Some native speakers of English see foreign languages as weapons in a war on the "American way of life." Carlos Alberto Montaner is editorial page editor of a Spanish newspaper in Miami and himself a native of Cuba. In 1988, he wrote about walking with his wife in Miami Beach, speaking Spanish and being told by a woman, a total stranger, "Talk English. You are in the United States." Montaner notices that the "expression on her face, curiously, was not that of somebody performing a rude action, but of somebody performing a sacred patriotic duty."[14]

Hispanics are not the only target of native-born Americans who are quick to suspect that those who speak another language are not "real" Americans because they don't use English and only English. When Frank Arcuri, a resident of Monterey Park, California, got upset in 1988 by the number of business signs in Chinese in his community, he didn't just criticize the confusion that English-speakers experienced in not being able to read the signs. Instead, Arcuri questioned whether the Chinese business-owners were trying to tear the community apart. "Let's put America first," he told the public in a meeting in Monterey Park. He continued:

> *Our city has bent over backwards long enough in an effort to accommodate our new immigrants.... They must adapt to our ways. They must use our language and respect our culture.... This is America; don't divide us. Don't isolate us by building a separate nation with your language and customs.*[15]

This hostility towards non-English speakers often goes hand-in-hand with hatred of anyone who is different. Hateful words can be powerful weapons against someone just learning English, and sometimes the victim doesn't have the words to combat it. A teenager named Lamthiane Inthirath, from the southeast Asian country of Laos, has written about her encounter with some boys in study hall during her freshman year of high school. They called her "Chink," an insulting word for someone from China; they didn't even know what country she was from, but she looked and sounded different and that was enough for the bullies. Lamthiane remembers that they laughed and threw cookies at her. "I realized that I was different, but I did not expect other students to treat me like that," she writes. "I got up rapidly without giving the boys a chance to move from their seats. I threw my math book in one of the boys' face." It was the boys, not Lamthiane, who received detention. After that, she writes, "they realized I had the same feelings as others, they made an apology and it was accepted. Shortly we became friends."[16]

Immigrants are forever changed by the experience of coming to America, and they usually exchange language, customs, and even attitudes for those of their new home. But the United States has also been changed by the new arrivals. In the next chapter, we will see how immigrants and their native languages have been treated in the history of our country.

Immigrants and the English Language in America

It was not clear for over a century after Europeans began to colonize North America in the early 1600s that English would be the majority language here. Spanish, French, German, Dutch, and English were all spoken by large groups of people in different parts of the continent. The language used depended on which European power held control over that area of the continent and where European settlers chose to live.

The English Language from Colonial Times to the Twentieth Century

The only people native to North America during this period of settlement were Native Americans. Some European missionaries learned Native-American languages in order to convert them to Christianity, and French missionaries began teaching the Native Americans French as early as 1604.[1] Some colonial traders also learned to speak with Native Americans either by teaching them European languages or by picking up their languages. There was a widespread attitude among the new arrivals, though, that Native Americans were "savages" with "primitive" languages, and many of the early settlers believed it was impossible to share European ideas of civilization with Native Americans. Many Native Americans were killed or driven west by expanding European settlements, and dozens of native languages were wiped out as native speakers of them died off. Even during the early twentieth century, many Native-American children were taken from their parents at an early age and put into special schools that forced them to leave their native languages and customs behind and learn the English language and new American customs.

Europeans also brought African slaves to the North American colonies almost from the beginning of settlement there. These unwilling "immigrants" were forced to give up many different African languages they spoke to make it easier for their masters to give them orders and to control them. But slaves were forbidden to learn to read and write in English, and states that allowed slavery into the nineteenth century usually made it a crime to teach them written English.

In the colonies that became the original thirteen states of the United States, English and German speakers were the two largest groups, with many of the German settlers in Pennsylvania. Germans made up 33.3 percent of the population in 1790. Even though the English and German colonists were very similar in appearance, there was still a lot of suspicion of the Germans among those with English backgrounds. Benjamin Franklin had printed some of the first North American books and newspapers in German in the 1730s. But this famous patriot and author later wrote of the "swarthy" [dark-skinned] Germans who "will never adopt our Language or Customs, any more than they can acquire our Complexion" and warned that English speakers would soon find living in Pennsylvania like living in a foreign country.[2]

In 1755 a Pennsylvania educator named William Smith described the benefits that the Germans could expect if they learned English in the schools he was setting up for them. He sounded very much like the Official English supporters quoted in the last chapter when he wrote that Germans who know English will qualify for "all the Advantages of native English Subjects....[By speaking English,] they may expect to rise to Place of Profit and Honor in the Country."[3]

When the colonies began to rise up against English rule by joining together in the Articles of Confederation in 1770, they published the Articles not only in English, but in German and French as well, hoping to gather support among as many colonists as possible. But once the colonies had won the revolution against England and become the United States of America, sentiment began to grow for using only English in the workings of government. In the 1790s, Congress voted to publish all present and future laws only in English.

Elsewhere in the country, there were large areas where English was a minority language. When Louisiana became a state in 1812, three-quarters of the population was French and the original state constitution was distributed in both French and English. In fact, Bernard Marigny, a French American, complained in 1845 about the increase in English speakers since Louisiana statehood. He grumbled that the English had "invaded everything" and boasted to the newcomers, "We could have become Americans without you."[4]

Spanish speakers were common in the nineteenth century in states in the southeast of the country like Louisiana and Florida, and they made up a majority in many parts of the southwest including sections of Texas and southern California. Anti-Hispanic feelings appeared as part of a movement known as "nativism" which opposed immigration, especially by Catholics.

One nineteenth century political party active in the 1850s that supported nativism, and opposed further immigration by Mexicans into the American southwest, was known as the "Know-Nothings." (They got their name from the fact that the members denied knowing anything about the party's activities.) The Know-Nothings pushed for restricting the use of Spanish and other languages in California. Nativists worked to maintain California's difficult literacy requirements for voting in hopes of keeping most Hispanics and Chinese Americans from taking part in the political process.

Language was not the only issue for the nativists. In fact, the Irish, who made up one of the largest immigrant groups in the nineteenth century and almost all spoke English as their native language, were despised by many Protestant Americans for their Catholicism. In addition, Irish newcomers to cities in the northeast would often find the letters "NINA." (*No Irish Need Apply*) written on boardinghouse doors and employee-wanted signs. African Americans, Asian Americans, and Native Americans all found limited job opportunities and sometimes met with violent hostility in many parts of the country, no matter how well they spoke English. Complaints over immigrants not learning and using English often served as a patriotic and acceptable mask for racism, religious intolerance, or the self-interest of immigrants' children who wanted to shut the door behind them on newcomers.

By the beginning of the twentieth century, a number of Americans, including those who owned and ran businesses, realized that it was important both for the new immigrants and for commerce that newcomers master English. Many factories around the country began to offer free instruction to their workers in the English language and American customs. Reformers like Frances Kellor, a pioneer in immigration education, convinced business leaders that workers who understood English and had become citizens were less likely to cause strikes and other labor troubles. One executive, Samuel Rea, the president of the Pennsylvania Railroad, insisted that it was not enough for immigrants to learn English: they must totally assimilate (adjust themselves to the majority in order to "fit in"). He wrote in a pamphlet distributed by Kellor that newcomers must be persuaded "to give up the languages, customs, and methods of life which they have brought with them."[5]

פאריז דענטאל
פארלארס קא.

מיר מאכען מעהר צאחן ארבייט
א טאג ווי אנדערע דענטיסטען א
יאהר.
עס לוינט אונז צו מאכען דיא
בעסטע ארבייט ביליג.

צייהן נעצויינען פאזיטיוו אהן
שמערצען.

מאכט קיין מיסטייק אין דיא
אדרעסען וועט איהר וויסען אז
אייער צאהן ארבייט ווערט געמאכט
אין ריכטינגען פלאץ.
80 דעלענסי סטריט,
קארנער ארטשארד סטריט, ניו יארק.
1815 מעדיסאן עוועניו,
קארנער 118טע סטריט, ניו יארק.
715 בראדווי,
נעבען פלאשינג עוועניו, ברוקלין.

This advertisement for a dentist from the early twentieth century uses both
English and Yiddish, the language spoken by many recently-arrived Jews
from Eastern Europe.

Conflicts over English in the Twentieth Century

It is an unusual fact that language conflict in the early twentieth century centered on the same ethnic group that caused so much concern to Benjamin Franklin in the eighteenth century: German Americans. In 1910, they were still the largest non-English-speaking group in the country: eight million German Americans, including two-and-a-half million immigrants supported over 550 German-language publications in the United States, as well as hundreds of social and artistic groups, athletic associations, and academic institutions.[6]

When the United States entered World War I against Germany in 1917, the general tolerance for the German language and German customs in America suddenly changed to suspicion and fear. German words like *sauerkraut* and *hamburger* were replaced in daily speech by "liberty cabbage" and "Salisbury steak"; even *German measles* became "liberty measles" for a time. Lawmakers were so afraid of spies among German Americans that even speaking German in public places or on the telephone became a crime. It is estimated that as many as eighteen thousand people in the Midwest alone were charged with violating laws that supported using only the English language.[7] Libraries cleared the shelves of books in the hated language, study of German as a foreign language was restricted, and even German-language religious services were forbidden. Newspapers like *The New York Times* supported anti-German legislation as "a matter...of patriotism, of Americanism."[8]

Even after the United States and its allies defeated Germany and its supporters in 1919, many states continued to pass laws designed to suppress the German language and force German speakers to assimilate to American ways and only use English. Oregon, for example, passed a law requiring that foreign-language publications could only be published in that state if they contained prominent, literal English translations of every article. Many of these statutes were reversed or struck down by the courts as unacceptable obstacles to the free speech guarantee in the first amendment to the Constitution of the United States. Still, German never regained its former position as a language of instruction and cultural unity for the millions of German Americans who had met with such hostility during World War I.

During the nineteenth century, when the United States was expanding in territory and Americans were building railroads, raising crops, mining minerals, and building up industries at an ever-increasing rate, a constant stream of immigrants was necessary. Unless the workforce kept increasing, there would not be enough Americans to lay the train tracks, plow the fields, dig up the iron and gold, and operate the textile machines and steel foundries that kept the nation growing.

Irish, Italian, Mexican, East European, Chinese, and people from dozens of other countries heard the rumors of "streets paved with gold" in America and often gave up everything they had to make sometimes dangerous journeys to the

These immigrant women from Europe are learning English and patriotism at a class in New York City in the early 1900s. They were among the lucky ones who were allowed to come to this country, seeking a better life.

United States. Chinese were denied the chance to immigrate to the United States starting in 1882, and Japanese immigration to this country, already limited, was stopped by the Immigration Act of 1924. Not until the 1950s were any but a few Asian immigrants permitted into America and only in the 1970s were large numbers allowed to enter this country.

After World War I, America started to restrict the number of other new immigrants, as well. Increasingly, many Americans came to believe the newcomers were "troublemakers" who took jobs away from "native" Americans, caused crime, and didn't share the ideals of the nation. Religious intolerance was also involved in the decision, since the limitations were especially severe on immigrants from Catholic countries and eastern Europe, the home of many Jews.

In 1920, the United States Senate passed a bill that, among other things, required aliens (non-citizens) under the age of forty-five who did not speak English to learn the language or be expelled from the country. The bill's sponsor, William S. Kenyon of Iowa, argued that the measure was necessary as a "step toward getting a nation of 110 million people to act and think without a foreign accent."[9] The bill carried a price tag of $12.5 million for the states to conduct the English-language classes, however, and the House of Representatives voted the bill down. Not until 1970 would Congress consider English-language legislation again.

Not everyone was so hostile to the immigrant at this time, and some showed an approach that closely resembles the kind of bilingual education programs in use today. In 1922, the

Children waiting for their parents to get permission to enter the United States posed around 1910, with American flags in an "Uncle Sam" wagon on Ellis Island. This was the entry point for over twelve million immigrants between 1892 and 1924. Most of the people coming into the United States at that time were European.

educator Sarah T. Barrows observed that kindergarten children who did not speak English were simply ignored in the classroom unless they learned enough English by sitting and listening to participate. Many of the children were unable to pick up English this way. She supported a different approach: giving the students "a thorough foundation in English before requiring as much of them as is expected from children of American parents."[10] Barrows believed that bilingual (two-language) children actually had an advantage over those who only knew English, but she proposed that teachers use kindergarten to change their students' "mother tongue" to English, while letting them keep the speech they used at home as a "foreign" language.[11]

The method of using only English to teach foreign language-speaking children is now known as the immersion method of language instruction: students are "immersed" (dipped or plunged into English like a nonswimmer into water) until they start to understand what they hear. Throughout the twentieth century, most schools continued to use the immersion method: it was the least expensive (no bilingual teachers were necessary) and, after all, it appeared to have worked for generations of immigrants from all over the globe. However, the drop-out rate for non-English-speaking students has been high, and many students with great abilities but no English were considered "slow" and put in classes where little was expected of them.

Throughout our history, the classroom has been the place where immigrant children became Americans, and generations of students who began as Italians, Russians, Mexicans, Greeks, Chinese, and other nationalities have found their way into the mainstream by learning the English language and American customs and values in school. Immigrants who don't speak English are still arriving in the United States, and in the next chapter we will look at some of the problems young immigrants face in adjusting to American society and the English language.

The Young Immigrant in America

Children are usually able to pick up a new language more quickly than their parents. This is, of course, a good thing for the child. But it can lead to problems when a member of the family, usually someone older, lags behind the children or spouse in picking up English.

Inside the Immigrant Family

Traditionally, the father in many Hispanic families has been "el jefe de la casa" (head of the household) and his wife was expected to look to him for answers. In turn, the children were expected to listen to their mother and father and obey them. What happens to a boy when his parents have to struggle just to make themselves understood in a new country with a new language? And what does the boy sacrifice as he becomes more American?

Richard Rodriguez, the Mexican-American author of

Hunger of Memory, remembers the embarrassment and fear he felt as a child of Spanish-speaking parents trying to make their way in an English-speaking society:

> *In public, my father and mother spoke a hesitant, accented, not always grammatical English. And they would have to strain—their bodies tense—to catch the sense of what was rapidly said by the gringos [non-Hispanic native Americans]....[I]t was unsettling to hear my parents struggle with English. Hearing them, I'd grow nervous, my clutching trust in their protection and power weakened.*[1]

Rodriguez also describes the changes that occurred in his family because his mother improved her English faster than his father. "On official business, it was [my mother], not my father, one would usually hear on the phone or in stores, talking to strangers," he recalls, and he describes how his father "retired into silence" when he had to speak English. The father stopped being head of the household in some ways because he was afraid or ashamed to speak English, but Rodriguez remembers how his father's voice would come alive when he spoke Spanish: "With firm Spanish sounds, he conveyed confidence and authority English would never allow him."[2]

Richard Rodriguez also remembers the conflicting pressures on him, on the one hand to keep the Mexican heritage that connected him to his family and, on the other hand, to assimilate (fit into American culture by using English and acting more like Americans). The teacher at Rodriguez's elementary school visited the family in their house and persuaded his parents to speak more English at home, and he began improving in the new language. Soon he was even thinking in English.

Unfortunately, Rodriguez's Mexican relatives were shocked at his poor Spanish. They blamed his parents for letting the boy lose his mother tongue. And they teased him by calling him *pocho* (a Hispanic who has forgotten his roots). He felt torn in opposite directions and his confusion affected his speech. Speaking in Spanish, he recalls, "A powerful guilt blocked my spoken words....I would speak, or try to speak, Spanish, and I would manage to utter halting, hiccupping sounds that [showed] my unease."[3] Only when Rodriguez started to study Spanish as a foreign language in high school did his nervous stutter in Spanish disappear.

Embarrassment, shame, guilt, and confusion are common emotions in any childhood. But Richard Rodriguez's story shows what powerful feelings were involved in one boy's journey from the private, familiar sounds of his native language to his mastery of English (and, finally, Spanish as well). He firmly believes that he has been able to achieve success in his life by learning English and using it as much as possible while he was growing up. But his story also shows the "private cost to be paid for public success,"[4] a cost that includes at least some isolation from members of his own family.

Problems with language in the immigrant family can arise not only between children and parents, but also between sisters and brothers of different ages when they assimilate to American ways at different rates. Vibora Lim, a girl from

Cambodia, arrived with her family in the United States in 1975 and settled in Boston a few months later. Lim's older sister and mother kept up their native language, Khmer, after Lim and her little brother began to learn English in school and use it nearly all the time.

Lim remembers that "When we first arrived in America, I knew how to read, write, speak and think in Khmer. Now...the only thing that I can write in Khmer is my first name." Lim describes the confusions that arise from the different ways family members express themselves: "It has been difficult for us to express our ideas, concerns, and feeling toward one another," she writes. "We often misinterpret each other, which results in conflict."[5] In Lim's family, using English was only one of the issues between older and younger members of the family that caused difficulties, but it caused divisions in the family when they most needed each other for support as they adjusted to the life and language of their new country.

The Young Immigrant Among Friends

Young people, especially teenagers, want desperately to "fit in" with their classmates and friends. For the young immigrant, this can present special problems, since even a casual chat can seem like an obstacle course when someone is embarrassed by a foreign accent and has to struggle to put strange sounds together into a sentence. Sometimes the customs of the young immigrant's home country can add to the difficulties of fitting into the crowd—and of learning English.

Chanthouk Ros came to the United States from Cambodia as a teenage girl. In Cambodia, girls were expected to be quiet and not to go out with friends unless adults were around. When she arrived in an American school in 1984, she remembers, "I looked like a dumb person because I didn't know any English....Most students thought of me as an isolated person, so no one ever wanted to speak to me at all....I had no friends except for my family."[6]

Ros had to get up her courage not only to talk to her classmates, but also to convince her parents to let her go out with her friends without her parents' supervision. Her courage paid off. The other students changed their mind about the "dumb" girl from Cambodia and began to accept her. Soon she had friends who helped her with English, encouraged her to speak up and not be so shy, and made her familiar with American customs. In Ros's case, she needed to start talking English in order to make friends. And she needed to make friends whom she could talk with in order to learn English.

Young people just coming to America can also find help in adjusting to all the changes they find by learning from other recent arrivals from the same background. Madelin Tellez, a thirteen-year-old junior high school student who had come to Oceanside, California, from Mexico, remembers what it was like to come to America without knowing any English. Luckily, she says, "There are other kids here from Mexico, so I don't feel lonely and it's easy to make friends."

Classes at her school are conducted in English and Spanish, so she is able to keep up with the other kids.

Tellez made friends with a girl from Mexico in the eighth grade who had been in the United States longer than Tellez had. The friends shared many activities, including bicycle riding, skating, and listening to music. Tellez and her friend also shared two languages, and when they're together they switch from Spanish to English and back again. In her new friend, Tellez found someone she can chat with in her native language and who can help her practice English and learn about the life of an American teenager.

Young Immigrants, Assimilation, and Language

It is difficult to make generalizations about young immigrants because their backgrounds and circumstances are so different, whether the subject is language, assimilation, or success in school. A high school student who has just fled with his parents from poverty in El Salvador, for instance, may not feel any closeness with another Spanish-speaking teenager who is the son or daughter of a wealthy Cuban-American family that arrived here a couple of decades ago. A Chinese-American girl in junior high school in San Francisco's Chinatown who hears and uses her native language every day may not have much in common with another Chinese-American teenager, living in a small town in the Midwest, who is the only Asian student in her school.

According to a study of immigrants' children published in

1993, there are tremendous differences in language use among different immigrant groups. Among all groups, the knowledge of English was strong: 80 percent of the five thousand teenage children of immigrants interviewed said their knowledge of English was good or very good. But 94 percent of Cuban-American students at private schools reported that they preferred English over their native Spanish while only 44 percent of the Mexican-American teenagers preferred English.[7] One explanation for this difference may be that the Cuban-American teenagers attending private schools received a better education in English than the Mexican Americans and therefore felt more comfortable speaking and writing it.

The two Hispanic groups were more similar when asked about speaking their parents' native language. Over 80 percent of Cuban-American and Mexican-American teenagers said they spoke good or very good Spanish. On the other hand, only about 30 to 40 percent of the Haitian-American, Filipino-American, and Vietnamese-American students said they spoke their parents' native language well or very well.[8] Hispanic Americans may keep their native language longer than other groups because new Spanish-speaking immigrants keep coming to the country and because Mexico and other Spanish-speaking countries are so close at hand. Filipino-American and Vietnamese-American teenagers, for instance, are less likely to travel back to their parents' homeland, and so they may assimilate more quickly and lose the language their parents spoke at home.

Many Hispanic Americans have kept their native language

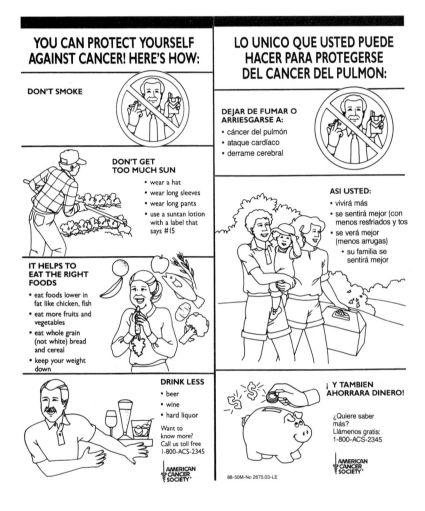

YOU CAN PROTECT YOURSELF AGAINST CANCER! HERE'S HOW:

DON'T SMOKE

DON'T GET TOO MUCH SUN
- wear a hat
- wear long sleeves
- wear long pants
- use a suntan lotion with a label that says #15

IT HELPS TO EAT THE RIGHT FOODS
- eat foods lower in fat like chicken, fish
- eat more fruits and vegetables
- eat whole grain (not white) bread and cereal
- keep your weight down

DRINK LESS
- beer
- wine
- hard liquor

Want to know more?
Call us toll free
1-800-ACS-2345

AMERICAN CANCER SOCIETY®

LO UNICO QUE USTED PUEDE HACER PARA PROTEGERSE DEL CANCER DEL PULMON:

DEJAR DE FUMAR O ARRIESGARSE A:
- cáncer del pulmón
- ataque cardíaco
- derrame cerebral

ASI USTED:
- vivirá más
- se sentirá mejor (con menos resfriados y tos
- se verá mejor (menos arrugas)
- su familia se sentirá mejor

¡ Y TAMBIEN AHORRARA DINERO!

¿Quiere saber más?
Llámenos gratis:
1-800-ACS-2345

AMERICAN CANCER SOCIETY®

88-50M-No 2675.03-LE

Anti-smoking information is as important to those who only speak Spanish as it is to those who can understand the warnings only in English. Organizations like the American Cancer Society use both languages to get out the message not to smoke.

longer than other immigrant groups. Because they make up the largest non-English-speaking group in the United States, many Spanish-speaking Americans, young and old, feel a special pride in their heritage. Puerto Ricans may move between San Juan and New York City, equally at ease with Spanish and English. Many, like Richard Rodriguez, whose story began this chapter, choose to make the sacrifices necessary to fit into mainstream American society and try for success in the English-speaking world at large, while remaining able to speak and write in their parents' language.

Guilienne Audelin, a fifteen-year-old Haitian American living in New York City, is able to speak excellent Creole, the language she grew up with, but she prefers "proper English." Audelin lives among other Haitian Americans in a poor neighborhood in New York known as Little Haiti. She is dark-skinned, like most Haitians, and she believes that mainstream society sees her color and assumes she's a "dummy."

"In America, [people] won't accept you for who you are. They look at the color of your skin, how you are dressed and how you look," she told an interviewer. The last thing she wants to do is to let other people's stereotypes limit her. Audelin says, "I am proud of my blood," but she does not want to be restricted to a life in Little Haiti, among other Creole speakers. Guilienne Audelin has had to make some hard choices: to ignore what "people" think and try for success; to maintain the pride she feels in her heritage, but not be limited by it; and to overcome economic hardship and the difficulties of life in an inner-city neighborhood to try to reach a difficult objective—becoming an American judge.[9]

Every young immigrant who comes to the United States pays a price for adjusting to the American way of life. For Richard Rodriguez, born in Mexico, assimilation meant becoming isolated from his family and their traditions. For Chanthouk Ros, from Cambodia, it meant going against the customs of the country where she was raised in order to fit into a circle of new American friends. Haitian-American Guilienne Audelin has had to fight against society's low expectations for her, keeping pride in her heritage while relying on "proper English" and education to reach her goal. Perhaps the immigrant dream of becoming part of American society while remaining distinct and special is a difficult one. But young people who are trying to make that dream come true are arriving in the United States every day.

The English-Only Movement Since 1980

"America is a nation of immigrants, but Americans have never really liked immigration,"[1] according to Charles Lane, a senior editor for *The New Republic* magazine. Given the history of the United States towards different immigrant groups (see Chapter 3), Lane's statement has a lot of truth to it. Still, the 1970s marked a turning point in American attitudes towards immigrants and towards the use of languages other than English in the United States.

Immigration in the 1970s

Perhaps the main reason that the 1980s became a decade of conflict over the place of English in American society was that immigration—both legal and illegal—reached record numbers in the 1970s. An estimated four million legal and eight million illegal immigrants arrived in the United States from 1970 to 1980.[2] Among the largest groups were Mexicans,

Cubans who were fleeing from Castro's communist dictatorship, and refugees from southeast Asia who came to the United States after the Vietnam War.

By 1980, Americans with English as their native language had become minorities in parts of southern Florida, in some communities in California, and elsewhere. In time, some people started to talk about the "immigration time bomb" that they believed would blow American society apart as legal and illegal immigrants took jobs away from Americans and made some natives feel like strangers in their own land.

The Debate Begins: Dade County, Florida, and the English Language Amendment (ELA)

Dade County, Florida voters decided in 1980 that English should be the official language there. The English-only ordinance remained in effect for thirteen years with only minor modifications made in 1983. "County officials [were]...forbidden by law to post a sign, translate a meeting, print a form, or distribute a pamphlet in Spanish, to subsidize a Hispanic arts festival, or to allow Spanish-language programming on the community-access cable T.V. channel,"[3] as the situation was described by James Crawford in his 1992 book *Hold Your Tongue: Bilingualism and the Politics of "English-Only."* Dade County includes the city of Miami, where the Hispanic population has expanded from 5 percent in 1959 to 62 percent in the early 1990s.[4] This is due mostly to the arrival of refugees from Cuba. Many Hispanics in Florida saw the ordinance not as a step towards ethnic unity but as a slap in the face to the rising prominence and power of Cuban Americans in the life of the state.

In 1981, Senator S.I. Hayakawa of California argued on the Senate floor that an amendment should be added to the United States Constitution making English the official language of the country (English Language Amendment or ELA). Senator Hayakawa, a Japanese American whose family had immigrated to the United States from Canada, believed that a common language was necessary for Americans to maintain their unity. "It is with a common language that we have dissolved distrust and fear," he asserted in a speech printed in 1985 and went on to argue that "...political differences become hardened and made immeasurably more difficult to resolve when they are accompanied by differences of language...."[5] For the sake of national unity and peace between different ethnic and language groups, Hayakawa wanted to bring the growth of "Hispanic language rights" to an end and establish once and for all that the United States was an English-speaking country and that citizens needed to learn English if they wanted to participate in the political process. The English Language Amendment was never passed by either the Senate or the House of Representatives.

"U.S. English," Bilingual Education, and Proposition 63

Senator Hayakawa found an ally in his fight for making English the official language of the country in Dr. John Tanton. He was an eye doctor in Michigan who headed up the Federation for American Immigration Reform (FAIR), a group that worked to stop the flow of illegal immigrants and to lower the number of legal immigrants allowed into the country each year. Together, Hayakawa and Tanton created "U.S. English" in 1983. The group lobbied the federal government to pass Hayakawa's Constitutional amendment. It would make English the official American language, repeal laws allowing ballots to be printed in languages other than English, and make sure that bilingual education programs were only short-term "stepping stones" that quickly prepared students for all-English instruction. U.S. English proved to be a successful lobbying group until a memo from Dr. Tanton surfaced in 1988. The memo exposed a nasty, racist side to the group's founder and caused well-known supporters of U.S. English to resign in protest. (See Chapter 1.)

Even with this setback, the U.S. English program found a good deal of support in many places around the country. In 1984 alone, three states passed laws making English their official language. In Tennessee, for instance, legislation was approved that required that all official documents be printed in English and no other languages could be used for ballots or in the public schools (except where the nature of the course would require otherwise—such as in foreign language courses).

President Ronald Reagan's Secretary of Education, William J. Bennett, gave a speech in September of 1985 in which he attacked the requirement that schools use bilingual education for non-English-speaking students and argued for more "flexibility" in trying other methods with the students. Bennett said in his speech that the "rise in ethnic consciousness...[and] ethnic pride in recent decades is a healthy thing," but that schools should not sacrifice mastery of English to the goal of making students proud of their different heritages, as he believed was happening.[6]

In 1986, 73 percent of California voters approved "Proposition 63," which made English the official language of the state and even allowed citizens there to sue government officials who acted to lessen or ignore the place of English as the common language of the state. The California measure received a great deal of publicity and the next year, no fewer than thirty-seven states considered "Official English" measures and five state legislatures passed English-language laws. Also in 1986, Larry Pratt, a former state representative in Virginia, formed "English First." The fund-raising letter used by English First warned that many immigrants were refusing to learn English and were "living off welfare and costing working Americans millions of tax dollars every year."[7] The Congress passed an immigration reform bill in 1986 that allowed some illegal immigrants already in the country to apply for legal status. One of the provisions of the bill was that those who wanted to become legal immigrants had to demonstrate that they were able to speak and write at least some English. The new immigration laws also strengthened the forces used to patrol the border between Mexico and the United States in an effort to keep further illegal immigration to a minimum.

"English Plus" and the End of the 1980s

During the mid-1980s, Americans on the other side of the English-language debate began to organize themselves. In 1985, the Spanish-American League Against Discrimination (SALAD) came up with the phrase "English Plus" to emphasize that programs like bilingual education were not set up to deprive students of instruction in English but to give them an opportunity to keep their own language while learning a second one. English Plus emphasized the need for *all* Americans to improve their skills in more than one language. The English Plus Information Clearinghouse (EPIC) was created in 1987 to support alternatives to the goals of the English-only movement. The EPIC "Statement of Purpose" argued that "...the national interest can best be served when all members of our society have full access to effective opportunities to acquire strong English language proficiency [mastery] *plus* mastery of a second or multiple languages."[8]

In 1989, the New Mexico state legislature became the first to support the goals of English Plus and to endorse the rights of language minorities. In a resolution that did not have the force of law but did reflect the opinion of a majority of the state representatives, the New Mexico lawmakers voted that the spirit of "diversity-with-harmony" would serve the state best. Further, the resolution stated that in order to prosper into the next century, America "...needs both the preservation of the cultures and languages among us and the fostering of proficiency in other languages on the part of its citizens."[9]

Oregon and Washington state soon passed their own versions of English Plus resolutions.

A federal court in 1990 struck down Arizona's English-only constitutional amendment, which made it illegal for government workers to use languages other than English on the job, whether they were speaking to each other or to members of the public who did not speak English. The case was brought by Maria-Kelly Yniguez, a state insurance-claims manager, who believed her rights to free speech were being put in jeopardy by the amendment. Federal court Judge Paul Rosenblatt agreed. However, in 1993, an Arizona superior court judge ruled "Official English" to be acceptable, further clouding this already controversial issue.

The tremendous pressure to "do something" about uncontrolled immigration that sparked the English-language debate in the early 1980s has decreased with the passage of the 1986 bill that reformed the immigration process. It is probably no coincidence that the furor over making English the official American language has also died down since the late 1980s.

Many Americans are still uncomfortable just listening to people speak a language they can't understand on the street or seeing stores that have signs in Spanish, Chinese, or any of the more than three hundred languages that are spoken in the United States. A recent poll showed that six out of ten Americans want immigration to this country slowed down, with half the people polled agreeing with the idea that most immigrants cause problems in our society.[10]

Teachers have been giving instruction in reading and writing to children of the Khmer Village in Houston, Texas since 1981.

Thomas Weyr, in his 1988 book *Hispanic U.S.A.: Breaking the Melting Pot*, supports a middle ground between those who believe that language minorities should get government help to maintain their differences and others who want English to be the official American language. What he says of Hispanics also applies to those with native languages other than Spanish. "Direct, even push, Hispanics toward and into English," he writes, "but leave them their native tongue to use as a bridge. Otherwise they will use Spanish to build another wall around themselves in our society."[11]

The Bilingual Education Debate

The increased rate of immigration into the United States was not the only reason for the intense debate over English in the 1980s. The growth of bilingual education programs and changes in the approaches and goals of the programs in the 1970s also served to fuel much of the debate.

In 1968, Congress had passed the Bilingual Education Act, which enables students to learn subject matter partly in their own language and partly in English. By 1973, the federal budget for bilingual education had grown to 45 million dollars and supported programs in twenty-six different languages, including such little-known tongues as Yup'ik, Cree, and Chamorro.

In 1974, the Supreme Court had ruled, in a case called *Lau* v. *Nichols*, that San Francisco schools had failed eighteen thousand Chinese-American students by not offering them any special instruction in the English language. The Court wrote in its decision that "Students who do not understand English are effectively [shut out] from any meaningful education....We know that those who do not understand English are certain to find their classroom experience wholly incomprehensible [impossible to understand] and in no way meaningful."[1] The Supreme Court did not spell out how schools should deal with the problem. It insisted, however, that schools could not allow students who knew no English to "sink or swim". Too many of them were drowning from the system of neglect.

When Ronald Reagan became President in 1980, one of the first acts of his administration was to change federal regulations. Up until then, schools were required to use a bilingual approach in teaching students who only knew a language other than English. Reagan's Secretary of Education, William J. Bennett, announced that the old regulations were "harsh, inflexible...unworkable and incredibly costly....We will protect the rights of children who do not speak English well," he wrote, "but we will do so by permitting school districts to use any way that has proven to be successful...."[2]

In fact, by 1980 many bilingual education programs had gone beyond their original goals. In 1978, Congress had decided only to fund bilingual programs that prepared students for instruction in English. Still, some bilingual programs continued working to improve the children's command of the languages they were already speaking at home. Others concentrated on getting "immigrant children to learn about the civilization of Spain or China [and] about their ancestors' role as explorers or railroad builders...."[3] Many people who had supported the original bilingual education concept thought the programs should limit themselves to helping foreign-born students learn English. Secretary of Education William Bennett's move in this direction was a small thing by itself, but it was an important official action in a passionate struggle over bilingual education that has still not been resolved.

What Is Bilingual Education?

Bilingual education in the United States is, by definition, instruction that includes English plus another language.

When the Supreme Court decided in the 1974 *Lau* v. *Nichols* case that Chinese-speaking students in San Francisco could not be allowed to "sink or swim," they left it to local school boards to come up with better ways of teaching their non-English-speaking students. Different schools have come up with very different solutions as to how students just learning English can be best taught.

Immersion is the most limited approach. Almost all instruction is in English and the students pick up the new language by being exposed to it in the classroom. In some immersion classes, when students are unclear about a certain word or phrase, they can ask the bilingual teacher about it in their native language. But the teacher will make the explanation in English. Gradually, the students begin to ask their questions in English and in this way they improve their spoken skills. Sometimes, the teacher is not bilingual, however,

Bilingual education in the United States is, by definition, instruction that includes English plus another language. The second language can be anything from Chinese (shown here) to Russian. A high school student presents part of a lesson in Chinese. The study of Chinese is increasing as more immigrants from Asia arrive in America and trade increases between China and the United States.

or there may be students with different native languages in the same classroom. In these cases, the teacher must rely on so-called "body English," that is, acting out the meaning with gestures and using facial expressions or pictures to get the ideas across.

English as a Second Language (ESL) is a second approach. ESL tries to build on the English the students already know and is often used with students who may not share the same native language. ESL programs may use many different techniques to give students instruction, including songs and games. These are used to teach words and lessons that are likely to come up in classes that are taught in English. Students often begin by going to classes like music and art where only English is used, and they gradually reach the point where all their instruction can be in English.

Transitional Bilingual Education (TBE) teaches students all their academic subjects (mathematics, reading, science, history, etc.) in their native languages until they learn enough English to attend classes conducted only in English. Sometimes, bilingual education teachers help students keep and build on their knowledge of languages other than English, an approach known as Maintenance Bilingual Education (MBE) programs.

Two-way or dual language bilingual education goes one step further and, for instance, teaches Spanish-speaking students English in the same classroom as English-speaking students are learning Spanish. The goal is that all the students in the class will become bilingual. Spanish-speaking students

v *V*

va   ve   vi   vo   vu   vy

páv   so-va   vo-sa

vy   o-ves   le-vý

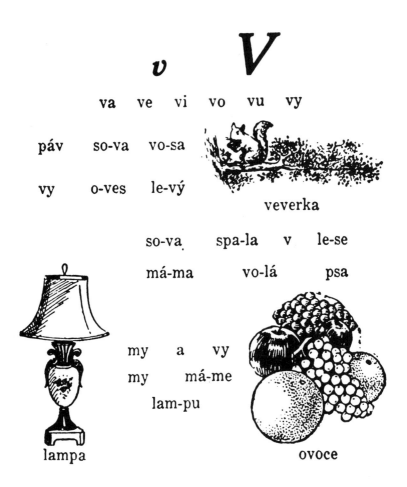

veverka

so-va   spa-la   v   le-se

má-ma   vo-lá   psa

my   a   vy

my   má-me

lam-pu

lampa   ovoce

Transitional Bilingual Education (TBE) teaches students all of their academic subjects (mathematics, reading, science, history, etc...) in their native language until they learn enough English to attend classes taught only in English. A page from a textbook in the Czech language is shown here. It is used in a school in Cedar Rapids, Iowa where children and adults have been taught in Czech since 1870.

in the two-way bilingual education classroom are valuable resources for their classmates who only speak English, and vice versa.

Bilingual / bicultural education not only uses the native language of foreign-speakers to teach them English, but also includes the history, culture, even the cooking and crafts that make up their special heritage. There is often an effort to make students proud of their backgrounds, since some students with little or no English may feel ashamed and embarrassed about their heritage.

There is still no agreement on what approach, or combination of approaches, works best with students just learning English. It may depend on how motivated the students are, how well they speak and write their native language, and how creative the teacher is in getting ideas across.

One argument against large-scale bilingual education programs is that they are too expensive. Sometimes, the needs of the native-born student cannot be met because too much of the education budget goes to hiring bilingual teachers and buying special materials for non-English-speaking students. In many cases, the money may simply not be there for both ambitious bilingual education programs and, for instance, reading tutorials for slow learners or special counseling for students with behavior problems.

As we have seen in previous chapters, there is also disagreement about what the ultimate goal of bilingual education should be. Some teachers, parents, and students believe that the most important thing is to get students as quickly as possible into classes that only use English. Some think it is just as important that students keep their native languages and even improve them as they are learning English. For others, the problem is that most American students can only speak one language—English.

Comparing Two Programs: A Dual-Language Bilingual Program at PS 84

New York, like Miami, Los Angeles, and many other American cities, is a city of many languages. Orthodox Jews in Brooklyn still speak Yiddish as their grandparents did when they came to America at the beginning of the century, while more recent Jewish arrivals from the former Soviet Union speak Russian. Haitians speak Creole. Recent Asian immigrants speak dozens of different languages and dialects.

However Spanish is by far the most common foreign language in New York City. At Public School (PS) 84 on West 92nd Street in Manhattan, only about half the students are Hispanic, but all students in a Dual-Language (DL) Bilingual Education Program there receive instruction in both Spanish and English.

The DL program runs from kindergarten to sixth grade and is totally voluntary. Nine of the twenty-five classes at PS 84 use the two-way bilingual approach and DL classes are usually evenly divided between Spanish-speakers and English-speakers. Classes are in one of the languages on alternate days: Monday, Spanish; Tuesday, English; etc. According to the principal of the school, Sidney H. Morison, "Neither English nor Spanish is taught....[C]hildren learn language as a by-product, through use."[4]

This approach may seem confusing. It sounds difficult for a student, especially at first, to have to remember what day it is to figure out what language to use in class. Young children adapt quickly to unusual situations, however, and teachers at PS 84 are careful not to criticize students who speak the "wrong" language. At the beginning of the DL program, English-speaking kindergarten students often answer "here" or "present" when their names are read during roll call at the beginning of class, and Spanish-speakers answer "presente" (the Spanish word for "here" or "present"). But listening to each other helps one group pick up the language of the other, according to Principal Morison. When a student asks in Spanish to go to the lavatory on an "English day," the teacher simply says, "Oh, you want to go to the bathroom. OK, go ahead." The whole class gets a chance to hear an accurate translation of what the student has just said in a natural, pleasant way.

One positive effect of the DL program is that the students have shown sympathy and helpfulness to a classmate who is just learning the language that is native to him or her. Principal Morison reports that "Those who are or become bilingual often assume the role of translator, helping others even without being asked."[5] Students from both groups acquire authentic accents in each other's languages as well.

The academic progress of the students in this DL program

is impressive and the approach at PS 84 has produced genuine bilingual students. Principal Morison argues that research has shown "that children in bilingual classes that separated languages scored higher in both English and Spanish than children in bilingual classes that mixed languages," and he reports that all the children in the DL program have picked up both languages and shown improvement in reading and speaking both languages at each grade level.[6]

Alternatives to Bilingual Education in Newton, Massachusetts

Rosalie Pedalino Porter had been a Spanish bilingual teacher in the Puerto Rican community in Springfield, Massachusetts for five years when she began to lose faith in the whole concept of bilingual education as it was being taught in the late 1970s. She reports that, "My students, after five or six years in the bilingual program, were neither acquiring English literacy [ability to read in English] nor succeeding in mastering school subjects taught in English."[7] Porter decided in 1979 to take off a few years to do research in the latest developments in English as a Second Language (ESL) instruction. In 1980 she became director of bilingual and ESL instruction in the Newton, Massachusetts public education system.

Newton, Massachusetts is a well-to-do community near Boston that in 1980 had students from twenty-two different language backgrounds, the most common being Cantonese (a dialect of Chinese), Russian, Spanish, Japanese, and Hebrew.[8]

The bilingual and ESL programs Porter directed in Newton had three important features:

- *Early immersion for students in English, beginning before kindergarten, and as much contact for them with native English speakers as possible;*

- *Well-trained teachers and staff who understood cultural differences among the students and expected hard work and high achievements from them;*

- *Involvement of the students' parents to make sure they understood and were able to participate in the program.*

Before a student was even enrolled in the Newton programs, the family and students were interviewed to find out what language skills they had. The parents were also sent a handbook that explained what programs were available. The handbook was available in the six most common languages among the students. Participation in the programs was entirely voluntary. Since only about 350 of the 8,000 Newton students did not have English as a native language, certain schools were chosen for the bilingual and ESL programs to make sure that students in the programs were not "lost" among native English speakers.

The ESL program used games, plays, songs, and visual aids to help students understand the meanings of new words and ideas. Teachers in the students' other classes also got involved, constantly supplying the ESL teachers with information about what topics were coming up, so the students could concentrate on vocabulary that would help them understand lessons in English. For example, if a mathematics teacher was planning to cover geometric shapes in the coming weeks, the ESL teachers would teach students the English words for "square," "circle," "triangle," etc., *before* the words came up in the math class.

Porter is skeptical about bilingual programs that keep students out of classes taught in English for five, even seven years, as some programs in Boston have done.[9] However, students in the Newton programs may also choose to take classes with bilingual teachers. Even in the bilingual classrooms, English is used from the very first day of school in addition to the students' native language, and the goal is to move the children quickly into English-language classes.

The Newton schools also offered students and their parents a variety of special services, including an ESL summer school, after-school tutorials, and special events for all students, such as those that introduce the native English speakers to foreign language and culture. Teachers also train Newton high school students to tutor younger children in the programs, and the teenagers get credit for the teaching they do under close supervision from the teachers.

According to Porter, all of the students in the Newton programs "become bilingual, with full ability to use English, their second language, effectively in the regular classroom after a few years." In addition, students in the programs are less likely to cut class or to drop out of school altogether: 60

percent go on to higher education. Porter believes that "Newton has developed a model program that...[includes] the strongest elements of the immersion, ESL, and bilingual approaches."[10]

There may not be any one right answer to the question: "What method works best in teaching students with native languages other than English?" If students and their families think it is important for all Americans to be familiar with more than one language, the dual-language approach used at PS 84 in New York City may be a good approach. There, English and Spanish speakers can help one another learn a second language, and after a few years all students can speak and write two languages well. On the other hand, if students and parents think the most important thing is to get non-English-speakers to master English as quickly as possible, the Newton, Massachusetts, model program may be the answer.

One thing is clear. It takes special effort, training, and funds to do a good job of teaching any student, and it takes even more work and resources to make sure that students who don't speak English won't "sink" instead of "swim."

chapter 7

Language
and Everyday Life
in America

Miami's mayor in 1982 was Puerto Rican-born Maurice Ferré. In a newspaper interview in that year he made a prediction that surprised even some Hispanics. "Within ten years there will not be a word of English spoken [in Miami]...one day residents will have to learn Spanish or leave,"[1] he told a reporter from Florida's *Tampa Tribune.*

Employment and Education
of Language Minorities

Ferré's prediction did not come true, and English can still be heard on the streets of Miami. But in another interview, Ferré talked about how well a Spanish speaker could get along in Miami without ever learning English. In the interview that follows, the former mayor was not overstating the case when he told an interviewer about the many ways a Spanish-speaker could avoid having to speak English.

You can be born [in Miami] in a Cuban hospital, be baptized by a Cuban priest, buy all your food from a Cuban grocer...and pay for it all with a check from a Cuban bank. You can get all the news in Spanish—read the Spanish daily paper, watch Spanish TV, listen to Spanish radio. You can go through life without having to speak English at all.[2]

While English speakers in Florida may be frustrated by this situation, the state has in fact benefited in a number of ways from its multilingualism (being able to speak many languages). In the twenty-five or so years after 1960 (when the first Cuban refugees started to arrive), more than one hundred fifty foreign companies have set up offices in Coral Gables, Florida. Many were attracted by a Spanish-speaking workforce, and these companies hired over four thousand workers. They pumped $200 million back into the city's economy through these workers' paychecks.[3]

According to Steve Clark, a longtime politician in Dade County (which includes Miami), it is Hispanics who are largely responsible for the economic and cultural boom in southern Florida. Taxes in Dade County were paid on $1.5 billion in 1958. By the mid-1980s it had grown to almost $50 billion and "Hispanics have stimulated everybody. They've added to cultural activities, and exposed us to things we never knew existed. Hispanic thinking opened up communications to all of Latin America."[4]

Miami and Dade County are not typical of the economic situation of Hispanics in the country, however. The Cuban

Americans who contributed most to the economic growth in southern Florida were among the wealthiest and best-educated people in Cuba and had the most to lose when Castro came to power in 1959. Many were able to send their children to private schools, and these children usually learned English rapidly and were able to move into good jobs, many of which required mastery of both English and Spanish.

For many immigrant children from Mexico or Central America, the opportunities to learn English and have a chance at economic success were, at least until recently, very limited. And for those who have failed at learning English and getting an education, the results have been tragic. A study of Mexican-American inmates in California's San Quentin prison in the 1960s found a majority had so little education in any language that they could not even participate in the prison's job-training program. Only 2 percent of the 146 Mexican-American ex-prisoners surveyed a few years later had managed to complete high school.[5]

Of course most Hispanics, like most Americans, fall somewhere between the rich Cuban-American businesspeople of Miami and the prisoners at San Quentin. But Hispanic children still do not do as well in school as other American children. More drop out of school even though special language programs have been set up to help them make the transition to bilingualism. As Earl Shorris wrote in his 1992 book *Latinos: A Biography of the People*, "...so far, bilingual education has not, of itself, solved the educational problems of Latino children. If [the "sink or swim" approach] caused them to fail, bilingual education has not caused them to succeed."[6]

Hispanics still have higher unemployment rates than non-Hispanics and their family income is only 64 percent of the income for non-Hispanic families.[7] According to Harry Pachon of the National Association of the Latino Elected Officials, the lack of ability in English is the major reason for these grim economic statistics: "At the turn of the century, you could drop out of school at 14 and it didn't matter," he told an interviewer from *U.S. News and World Report* in 1987. He continued, "In today's technological society, English is a must."[8]

But the picture of Spanish-speaking Americans refusing to learn English and join mainstream society is an inaccurate one, according to James Crawford, the editor of the 1992 book *Language Loyalties: A Source Book on the Official English Controversy.* Crawford presents the following statistics, which paint a very different portrait of Hispanic Americans and their use of English. He notes that:

- *98 percent of all Americans over the age of four speak English "well" or "very well";*

- *Three out of four Hispanic Americans who have been in the United States for fifteen years or more speak English every day;*

- *Adult education classes in English for Hispanic Americans and other language minorities run twenty-four hours a day in cities like Los Angeles.[9]*

Members of language minorities—both Hispanic Americans and non-Hispanics—who have pushed themselves and their children hard to learn English and do well in school have met with a great deal of success in the United States. Ben J. Wattenberg, author of the 1990 article "The Case for More Immigration," notes that "of the 40 finalists in the 1988 Westinghouse high-school science competition, 22 were foreign-born or the children of foreign-born parents....In Boston, 13 of the 17 public-high-school [students getting the top grades in their grade] in the class of 1989 were foreign-born." And he quotes researchers at San Diego State University who report that "immigrants and refugees to the U.S.—whether from Asia, Europe, or Latin America—are systematically outperforming all native-born American students in grade-point averages despite...English-language handicaps."[10]

Asian Americans have often been singled out as "model minorities," and they make up a large percentage of students attending the top universities in the country. By the early 1980s, for instance, Asian Americans made up almost 15 percent of the students applying for admission at universities such as Brown, Harvard, Princeton, and Yale. The numbers of qualified Asian-American applicants were so great, in fact, that these and other universities have been accused of maintaining informal quotas on the number of Asian Americans accepted.[11] And as early as 1970, Chinese- and Japanese-American families both had higher average incomes than

Teenagers wait their turn to demonstrate their martial arts skills and perform a dragon dance to greet the Chinese New Year at a multicultural festival at a high school in Quincy, Massachusetts.

white Americans ($3,000 higher for Japanese Americans and $1,000 higher for Chinese Americans).[12]

Language Minorities and the Media

The English-language media in the United States have tended to simplify the situation of language minorities. One such example is portraying Asian Americans as model immigrants and Hispanic Americans as poverty-stricken ghetto-dwellers.

Linda Chavez, the writer and supporter of the English-language movement portrayed in Chapter 1, ran a computer search in 1990 of American newspapers and magazines. She found no fewer than twenty-five hundred stories that linked Hispanic Americans and poverty. She pointed out in an article in the newspaper insert *Vista* that is was wrong to put so much emphasis on the 26 percent of Latinos who are poor and virtually ignore the 74 percent who are not.[13]

The newspapers and magazines that report that Asian Americans are all-prospering and attending Ivy League colleges are just as misleading. Studies of Vietnamese refugees in California have shown that about half receive public assistance (welfare and other government programs) and even American-born citizens with a Filipino heritage only make about half the salary of American-born whites.[14] These statistics show a very different picture from the one people usually read about in the American English-language media. It shows that language barriers and ethnic prejudices have been obstacles to progress for Asian Americans, as for other minorities in this country.

Meanwhile, there has been a tremendous increase in media

available in this country in languages other than English. In addition to over five hundred radio and television stations that serve speakers of Spanish, Chinese, Korean, Russian, and dozens of other languages, newspapers and magazines in these and other languages are available in many large American cities. As early as 1970, for instance, there were eight Spanish-language newspapers published in Los Angeles County (including two dailies) and nine published elsewhere that were also available there. Residents of Los Angeles County could also choose among almost a dozen Spanish-language magazines, two of which were published in the county itself.[15] The number has increased dramatically since then.[16]

Some English-language newspapers have also reached out to language minorities by including supplements in other languages. Advertisers regularly use billboards and other promotional devices to reach consumers whose native language is not English. For instance, almost half the advertisements in New York City subways are in Spanish.[17]

Many local television and radio stations have put aside a certain amount of time each week to provide information and entertainment directed at language minorities. On these television programs, local personalities will often be interviewed in their native language while an English translation is provided by using subtitles. Conversations with English speakers on these programs will be translated into a second language in the same way. These subtitles can also be used by English speakers to pick up words and phrases in foreign languages, and non-English-speakers can learn English the same way.

Public television has worked hard to help English-speakers in the country become familiar with foreign languages and cultures. Since its early days, it has provided television courses in Spanish, French, Russian, and other languages.

Sesame Street, the educational children's series on public television, has been including Spanish-speaking performers and entertaining views of Hispanic culture since 1971. *Sesame Street* has also introduced Rosita (a Spanish-speaking muppet), and Celina (a Filipino-American woman who runs a dance studio) to make children familiar with language minorities. Linda Ronstadt has also performed traditional Mexican songs, and even Big Bird has picked up a few Spanish words that he shares with the audience.

Government Services and Health Care for Language Minorities

In 1975, the U.S. Congress gave language minorities help in participating in this country's political process when it passed several amendments to the 1965 Voting Rights Act. Written and spoken assistance for non-English speakers must be provided in counties where:

- at least 5 percent of potential voters spoke a single language other than English;

and *either* of the following situations apply:

- English literacy in a community was below the average for the country as a whole; and/or

Even Big Bird learns about Mexican culture and how to speak Spanish on *Sesame Street*. For over twenty-five years this educational program for kids has been offering American children images from the many cultures that make up America.

- English-language elections attract less than 50 percent of eligible voters.

Over three hundred counties fit these requirements, and most started to provide voting materials in languages other than English and bilingual voting assistants for Spanish speakers, Native Americans, Alaskan Natives, and Asian Americans. According to Vilma Martinez, president of the Mexican-American Legal Defense and Educational Fund, the Voting Rights Act amendments of 1975 provided the "beginnings of a fair share" for language minorities and, in fact, their participation in the voting process and their success in winning public office has shown dramatic increases since the 1970s.[18]

The Internal Revenue Service (IRS), which collects federal taxes, the Immigration and Naturalization Service, and many other government agencies at the national, state, and local levels have also taken steps to help non-English speakers with information and services in their languages. In California, with its large Hispanic-American and Asian-American populations, foreign-language materials have been produced that give information on everything from unemployment benefits and food stamps to Department of Health pamphlets and emergency and disaster relief. Motor vehicle laws, consumer rights information, and services for those seeking state grants to build housing have also been provided in Spanish and several other languages.

In addition, nongovernment agencies that want to reach out to the public have used languages other than English to reach as many Americans as possible. The American Cancer Society has used Spanish in its anti-smoking publications, conducted workshops for Hispanic Americans on cancer prevention and detection, and has even produced a Spanish-language waterproof "shower card" to help women examine themselves at home for breast cancer. Public service health messages are also carried in Spanish-language newspapers and television and radio stations. Hospitals and other health care providers have also taken pains to hire bilingual staff to make sure that non-English speakers receive appropriate care.

8

Striking the Right Balance

The debate over language in the United States has often been heated and sometimes nasty. Those who have defended the rights of language minorities have sometimes been quick to label their opponents as small-minded bigots. Opponents of Arizona's English-only constitutional amendment, for instance, used pictures of concentration camp victims behind barbed wire to suggest that supporters of the amendment were Nazis.[1]

Some supporters of making English the official language of the United States and limiting immigration have been just as quick to portray recent immigrants as dangerous threats to the unity of the country and troublemakers who exploit the generosity of the American system. For example, William J. Knight, a California assemblyman from a suburb near Los Angeles, circulated this offensive piece of verse against Hispanic immigrants to voters in his district in May of 1993:

"Everything is mucho good./Soon we own the neighborhood./We have a hobby—it's called breeding./Welfare pay for baby feeding."[2] Knight even mixed in a word of Spanish ("mucho" meaning "very") and used bad grammar ("welfare pay" instead of "welfare pays") to add ridicule to his insults.

But the argument over the place of English and other languages in this country has, for the most part, been fought with words. Elsewhere, debates over language have sometimes turned into bloody warfare. The speakers of Basque, a language used by a few hundred thousand people near the border of France and Spain, have used terrorist tactics in their fight for a separate Basque-speaking state. There have been riots in Belgium between speakers of French and Flemish. On the island of Sri Lanka, off the Indian coast, Sinhalese and Tamil speakers have often been involved in violence against each other in the last decade. Many died in India when speakers of different languages fought with each other in the 1950s and 1960s. Even Canada, which has a large French-speaking minority centered in the province of Quebec, saw government officials kidnapped in the cause of a separate, French-speaking Quebec in 1970.

These examples from other countries have been used by supporters of the U.S. English movement to show the potential for conflict that exists when different language groups fight each other for power. But opponents of making English the official language of the country make the argument that vigorous debate is very much in the American tradition and has rarely been the source of violence in this country.

In fact, nations like Switzerland have prospered and maintained their unity for centuries although *four* languages are officially recognized there: French, German, Italian, and Romansch. Most Swiss know at least two or three of these languages, in addition to English. For centuries the Swiss have been able to play a part in international commerce well beyond their numbers, in part because they speak the languages of many of their European and North American trading partners.

The Swiss and other Europeans who master several languages may have a lesson to teach Americans, who have traditionally been slow to learn foreign languages. One reason for Americans' reluctance to speak anything but English comes from the dominance of the language in over sixty countries around the world. More than 316 million people have English as their native language and nearly as many speak English as a second language. In addition, three-quarters of all mail is in English, as well as 80 percent of computer data input around the world.[3]

Still, knowing a foreign language can make doing business abroad much easier and sometimes means the difference between success and failure. Paul Hirsch, a retired business executive, told an interviewer in 1979 that "Dealing with the...foreign buyer of American goods in his local tongue can produce unexpected results, especially in pursuing new methods of trade....[C]omplicated case-by-case deals can best be [begun] and carried out on the spot . . . by negotiating in local languages."[4]

Frank A. Weil, former Assistant Secretary of Commerce

for Industry and Trade, makes a similar point when he observes that Americans sometimes fall behind Europeans and Asians in breaking into new markets because the Americans only know English: "Part of the reason the Japanese and the Germans sell so effectively is that they have gone to the trouble of learning about us and adapting the products they export to our tastes and markets....[Foreign] language promotion, like export promotion, would benefit the American business community and, in turn, our economy."[5]

Senator Paul Simon from Illinois wrote a book about the learning of foreign languages in the United States in 1980 called *The Tongue-Tied American: Confronting the Foreign Language Crisis*. In the book, he points to a number of disturbing facts, including the following:

- *Less than 20 percent of American high school students study foreign languages, compared to almost 40 percent in 1915 (with the number actually declining) and fewer than 4 percent of high school graduates have studied a foreign language for more than two years;*

- *One in five high schools in the country doesn't teach any foreign languages at all;*

- *There are few Americans studying some of the world's most popular languages: for example three hundred million people speak Hindi, mostly in India, but not even three hundred Americans were studying the language around 1980.*[6]

In Illinois Senator Paul Simon's 1980 book, *The Tongue-Tied American*, he pointed out that so few Americans speak a second language that perhaps we should greet visitors to the United States with a sign that says: WELCOME TO THE UNITED STATES - WE CANNOT SPEAK YOUR LANGUAGE.

Since Senator Simon collected these figures enrollment in high school foreign-language classes has steadily dropped. There was an over 13 percent decline between 1976 and 1985, and a further drop of over 8 percent between 1986 and 1990.[7] Furthermore, two-thirds of undergraduates receiving bachelor's degrees in the mid-1980s took no college foreign-language classes at all.[8]

Senator Simon has written, humorously but with a serious point in mind, that "We should erect a sign at each point of entry into the United States:—WELCOME TO THE UNITED STATES—WE CANNOT SPEAK YOUR LANGUAGE."[9] He has come up with almost one hundred suggestions for changing this situation. Among the steps he proposes are: incentives for teaching foreign languages should be given to local school boards; foreign-language speakers should be regular visitors to elementary and high schools; students who have a native language other than English should be encouraged to maintain and improve their skills in it; only students who have studied foreign languages should be admitted to college; and businesses with overseas operations should provide opportunities for college students to live abroad, working in the foreign offices of the company and picking up the local language.[10]

Some Americans are not waiting for foreign language programs to catch up with the needs that Senator Simon points out. Rosalie Pedalino Porter, the educator and author discussed in Chapter 6, writes that some American parents and teachers have set up so-called "Saturday schools" where children can work at maintaining their native language skills or learn their parents' or grandparents' language. "I have seen the Chinese in my own community providing one day a week of instruction in Mandarin language, as well as in Chinese music, dance, and poetry," she writes. "The Japanese weekend school in a nearby suburb offers reading, writing, and other school subjects taught in Japanese."[11]

The American Folklife Center at the Library of Congress in Washington, D.C., profiled over a dozen schools in the 1988 book *Ethnic Heritage and Language Schools in America.* The schools from around the country introduce students to languages and cultures that have been forgotten as their parents or grandparents adapted to the American way of life.

In the Khmer village in Houston, Texas, 150 Cambodian Americans have the opportunity to take part in cultural and language classes. According to one of the teachers there, for children who have been embarrassed in the English-speaking public schools, "The village school offers a haven in which they can feel productive....When they go back home they say, 'I know how to write in Cambodian!'"[12] The Cambodian language instruction also serves as a bond between generations. A teacher at the Khmer village told a researcher that, in one family, "the children have outgrown the mother....She can't communicate...they don't speak Cambodian and she doesn't speak English."[13] The Cambodian classes help students stay close to parents who find it too difficult to speak English.

The Czech School in Cedar Rapids, Iowa, has been around since at least 1870 and offers summer session classes divided into three grade levels. Materials include textbooks and song-sheets for learning the words to Czech folk songs. One of the students, a nine-year-old boy named Chris Ransom, first got interested in finding out about the language his grandparents spoke when they brought him to an "ice cream social" and graduation ceremony at the school. He was quick to pick up Czech vocabulary, and, when he gets home from class, he enjoys showing off his newfound knowledge to his father and older brother, neither of whom speak any Czech. Like most of the students, Chris's friends are mostly Americans from other backgrounds, but each summer he chooses to learn Czech and find out about the heritage that even other members of his family have lost touch with.[14]

Saturday and summer schools are probably not the answer to the problem of Americans' reluctance to learn foreign languages in the public schools and universities. However, the students who voluntarily enroll in these schools and give up their weekends and summers to learn a second language demonstrate that reluctance is far from universal. It may be an indication that, given the proper incentives, many more American students would take the trouble to become "citizens of the world" and gain an advantage in the international marketplace at the same time.

There is an African proverb that says "It takes an entire village to raise a child." One way of looking at the controversy over languages in the United States is to think of education as a way of making each child feel comfortable in the "village" of America—and of the world. There is no other reason to think that schools have to erase all the differences between us in order to make us one nation. After all, people come to America because it is "the land of the free." Perhaps it is common values more than a common language that binds us together as one country.

It is important that we are able to communicate with each other, however. New arrivals should learn English not because they won't be Americans otherwise, but because it is a necessary tool for them. On the other hand, Americans who only know English may be harming their own opportunities for success and are certainly shutting themselves out from the so-called "global village."

No one culture has made the nation what it is. Oscar Handlin, in his 1951 book *The Uprooted*, observes that "Once I thought to write a history of the immigrants in America. Then I discovered that the immigrants *were* American history."[15] All Americans may not speak the same language, although almost all of them do. But each wave of immigration to our country has brought a special point of view that adds to the richness of our nation.

Chapter Notes

Chapter 1

1. 1980 U.S. Census (cited in Frank L. Schick and Renee Schick, eds., *Statistical Handbook on U.S. Hispanics* [Phoenix, Oryx Press, 1991] p. 63.) found less than 3 million of the 11 million Americans who talked in Spanish at home could not speak English well or at all. The 1976 Hispanic Policy Development Project commissioned by Dr. Calvin Veltman (cited in Siobhan Nicolau and Rafael Valdivieso, "Spanish Language Shift: Educational Implications," in James Crawford, ed., *Language Loyalties: A Source Book on the Official English Controversy* [Chicago, The University of Chicago Press, 1992] p. 319.) estimated there were more than 3 million Americans of Hispanic descent who only spoke English.

2. According to *The Statistical Abstract of the United States* (Washington, D.C.: Government Printing Office, 1993), p. 51 (Table 57), about 1,547,000 Americans over the age of five speak Spanish at home. The next-largest group of Americans over five who speak languages other than English at home contains 1,309,000 people and covers speakers of all Asian and Pacific languages.

3. James Crawford, *Hold Your Tongue: Bilingualism and the Politics of "English Only"* (Reading, Mass.: Addison-Wesley Publishing Company, 1992), p. 79.

4. Joe Bernal, "I Am Mexican-American," *National Education Association Journal,* May 1969; reprinted as "Bilingual Education for La Raza," in Wayne Moquin and Charles Van Doren, eds. *A Documentary History of the Mexican Americans* (New York: Praeger Publishers, 1971), p. 369.

5. Ibid.

6. James Crawford, "What's behind Official English?" in James Crawford, ed., *Language Loyalties: A Source Book on the Official English Controversy* (Chicago: The University of Chicago Press, 1992), p. 172.

7. Crawford, *Hold Your Tongue*, pp. 155–156.

8. John Tanton, memorandum to "WITAN IV Attendees," October 10, 1986; quoted in Crawford, "What's behind Official English?" pp. 172–173.

9. Crawford, *Hold Your Tongue*, p. 157.

10. Linda Chavez, *Out of the Barrio: Toward a New Politics of Hispanic Assimilation* (New York: BasicBooks, 1991), p. 6.

11. Diane Telgen and Jim Kamp, eds. *Notable Hispanic American Women*, (Detroit, Gale Research Inc., 1993), p. 93.

12. Ibid., pp. 95, 93.

Chapter 2

1. S.I. Hayakawa, "The Case for Official English," in Crawford, ed., *Language Loyalties: A Source Book on the Official English Controversy* (Chicago: The University of Chicago Press, 1992), pp. 94, 100.

2. Richard D. Lamm and Gary Imhoff, *The Immigration Time Bomb: The Fragmenting of America* (New York: E. P. Dutton [Truman Talley Books], 1985), p. 111.

3. Ibid.

4. Walter Huddleston, "The Misdirected Policy of Bilingualism," in Crawford, ed., *Language Loyalties*, p. 115.

5. Jamie B. Draper and Martha Jiménez, "A Chronology of the Official English Movement," in Crawford, ed., *Language Loyalties: A Source Book on the Official English Controversy*, (Chicago: The University of Chicago Press, 1992), p. 90.

6. Lamm and Imhoff, p. 116.

7. Ibid., p. 117.

8. James Crawford, *Hold Your Tongue: Bilingualism and the Politics of "English Only"* (Reading, Mass.: Addison-Wesley Publishing Company, 1992), p. xii.

9. Draper and Jiménez, pp. 92–94.

10. Max J. Castro, "On the Curious Question of Language in Miami," in Crawford, ed., *Language Loyalties*, p. 179.

11. Shirley Achor, *Mexican Americans in a Dallas Barrio* (Tuscon, Ariz.: University of Arizona Press, 1978), p. 122.

12. Richard Rodriguez, *Hunger of Memory: The Education of Richard Rodriguez* (New York: Bantam Books, 1983), p. 19. "Luxury and Tragedy," quoted in Rosalie Pendalino Porter, *Forked Tongue: The Politics of Bilingual Education* (New York: BasicBooks, Inc., 1990), p. 9.

13. Porter, *Forked Tongue*, p. 220.

14. Carlos Alberto Montaner, "Talk English—You Are in the United States," in Crawford, ed., *Language Loyalties*, p. 163.

15. Crawford, *Hold Your Tongue*, p. 8.

16. Lamthiane Inthirath, "A Change of Cultures," in Lucy Nguyen-Hong-Nhiem and Joel Martin Halpern, eds., *The Far East Comes Near: Autobiographical Accounts of Southeast Asian Students in America* (Amherst, Mass.: The University of Massachusetts Press, 1989), p. 191.

Chapter 3

1. Paul Simon, *The Tongue-Tied American: Confronting the Foreign Language Crisis* (New York: Continuum, 1980), p. 13.

2. Dennis Baron, *The English-Only Question: An Official Language for Americans?* (New Haven, Conn.: Yale University Press, 1990), p. 66.

3. Ibid., p. 70.

4. Ibid., p. 85.

5. James Crawford, *Hold Your Tongue: Bilingualism and the Politics of "English Only"* (Reading, Mass.: Addison-Wesley Publishing Company, 1992), p. 56.

6. Ibid., p. 57.

7. Baron, p. 111.

8. Ibid., p. 110.

9. Ibid., p. 141.

10. Ibid., p. 153.

11. Ibid., p. 154.

Chapter 4

1. Richard Rodgriguez, *Hunger of Memory: The Education of Richard Rodriguez* (New York: Bantam Books, 1983), pp. 13, 15.

2. Ibid., pp. 24–25.

3. Ibid., p. 28.

4. Ibid., p. 35.

5. Lucy Nguyen-Hong-Nhiem and Joel Martin Halpern, eds., *The Far East Comes Near: Autobiographical Accounts of Southeast Asian Students in America* (Amherst, Mass.: The University of Massachusetts Press, 1989), p. 191.

6. Ibid., p. 125.

7. Deborah Sontag, "A Fervent 'No' to Assimilation in New America," *The New York Times*, June 29, 1993, p. A10, discussing research at Johns Hopkins University directed by Alejandro Portes.

8. Ibid.

9. Sontag, p. A10.

Chapter 5

1. David L. Bender, et. al., eds., *Immigration: Opposing Viewpoints* (San Diego, Greenhaven, 1990), p. 13.

2. Thomas Weyr, *Hispanic U.S.A.: Breaking the Melting Pot* (New York: Harper & Row Publishers, 1988), p. 26.

3. James Crawford, *Hold Your Tongue: Bilingualism and the Politics of "English Only"* (Reading, Mass.: Addison-Wesley Publishing Company, 1992), p. 91.

4. Ibid.

5. S.I. Hawakawa, "The Case for Official English," in James Crawford, ed., *Language Loyalties: A Source Book on the Official English Controversy* (Chicago: The University of Chicago Press, 1992) pp. 94, 100.

6. William J. Bennett, "The Bilingual Education Act: A Failed Path," in James Crawford, *Language Loyalties: A Source Book on the Official English Controversy* (Chicago: The University of Chicago Press, 1992), pp. 362-363.

7. James Crawford, "What's Behind Official English?," *Language Loyalties*, p. 173.

8. The English Plus Information Clearinghouse, "The English Plus Alternative," (Chicago: The University of Chicago Press, 1992), p. 152.

9. The New Mexico Legislature, "English Plus Resolution," (Chicago: The University of Chicago Press, 1992), section 1, p. 154.

10. Seth Mydans, "A New Tide of Immigration Brings Hostility to the Surface, Poll Finds," *The New York Times*, June 27, 1993, section 1, pp. 1, 16.

11. Weyr, p. 225.

Chapter 6

1. Dennis Baron, *The English-Only Question: An Official Language for Americans?* (New Haven, Conn.: Yale University Press, 1990), pp. 171-172.

2. Carlos J. Ovando and Virginia P. Collier, *Bilingual and ESL Classrooms: Teaching in Multicultural Contexts* (New York: McGraw-Hill Book Company, 1985), p. 228.

3. James Crawford, *Hold Your Tongue: Bilingualism and the Politics of "English Only"* (Reading, Mass.: Addison-Wesley Publishing Company, 1992), p. 76.

4. Sidney H. Morison, "A Spanish-English Dual-Language Program in New York City," in Richard D. Lambert and Alan W. Heston, eds., *English Plus: Issues in Bilingual Education* (Newbury Park, Calif.: Sage Publications, March 1990 [The Annals of the American Academy of Political and Social Science, vol. 508]), pp. 162–163.

5. Ibid., p. 166.

6. Ibid., p. 166–167.

7. Rosalie Pedalino Porter, "The Newton Alternative to Bilingual Education," (Newbury Park: Calif.: Sage Publications, 1990), p. 149.

8. Ibid., p. 150.

9. Rosalie Pedalino Porter, *Forked Tongue: The Politics of Bilingual Education* (New York: Basic Books, 1991), p. 6.

10. Ibid., pp. 139–140.

Chapter 7

1. Linda Chavez, *Out of the Barrio: Toward a New Politics of Hispanic Assimilation* (New York: Basic Books, 1991), p. 85.

2. Richard D. Lamm and Gary Imhoff, *The Immigration Time Bomb: The Fragmenting of America* (New York: E. P. Dutton [Truman Talley Books], 1985), pp. 91-92.

3. Thomas Weyr, *Hispanic U.S.A.: Breaking the Melting Pot* (New York: Harper & Row Publishers, 1988), p. 155.

4. Ibid.

5. Earl Shorris, *Latinos: A Biography of the People* (New York: W. W. Norton & Company, 1992), p. 176.

6. Ibid., p. 177.

7. Frank L. Schick and Renee Schick, eds., *Statistical Handbook on U.S. Hispanics* (Phoenix: Oryx Press, 1991), p. 203.

8. David Whitman, et. al., "For Latinos, a Growing Divide," *U.S. News and World Report*, August 10, 1987, p. 48.

9. James Crawford, ed., *Language Loyalties: A Source Book on the Official English Controversy* (Chicago: The University of Chicago Press, 1992), p. 171.

10. Ben J. Wattenberg, "The Case for More Immigration," in Robert Emmet Long, ed., *Immigration to the United States* (New York: The H. W. Wilson Company, 1992), p. 153.

11. Sucheng Chan, *Asian Americans: An Interpretive History* (Boston: Twayne Publishers/A Division of G. K. Hall & Co., 1991), pp. 179–180.

12. Ibid., pp. 168–169. Some researchers have pointed out, however, that more members of Chinese and Japanese-American families work than in white families. So their average *personal* income may, in fact, have been somewhat lower than for whites.

13. Shorris, p. 231.

14. Chan, p. 170.

15. The California Supreme Court, *Castro v. State of California*, in Crawford, *Language Loyalties*, p. 265.

16. James Crawford, *Hold Your Tongue: Bilingualism and the Politics of "English Only"* (Reading, Mass.: Addison-Wesley Publishing Company, 1992), p. 128.

17. Weyr, p. 189.

18. John Trasvina, "Bilingual Ballots: Their History and a Look Forward," in Crawford, *Language Loyalties*, p. 262.

Chapter 8

1. James Crawford, *Hold Your Tongue: Bilingualism and the Politics of "English Only"* (Reading, Mass.: Addison-Wesley Publishing Company, 1992) p. 161.

2. Robert Reinhold, "A Welcome for Immigrants Turns to Resentment," *The New York Times*, August 25, 1993, p. A12.

3. Dennis Baron, *The English-Only Question: An Official Language for Americans?* (New Haven, Conn.: Yale University Press, 1990), p. 178.

4. Paul Simon, *The Tongue-Tied American: Confronting the Foreign Language Crisis* (New York: Continuum, 1980), p. 28.

5. Ibid., pp. 28–29.

6. Ibid., pp. 2, 4.

7. United States Department of Education, National Center for Education Statistics, *Digest of Education Statistics* (Washington, D.C., 1993), p. 69.

8. United States Department of Education, National Center for Education Statistics, *The Condition of Education* (Washington, D.C., 1993), p. 75.

9. Ibid., p. 1.

10. Ibid., pp. 179–189.

11. Rosalie Pedalino Porter, *Forked Tongue: The Politics of Bilingual Education* (New York: Basic Books, Inc., 1990), p. 177.

12. Brett Topping, *Ethnic Heritage and Language Schools in America* (Washington, D.C.: The American Folklife Center at the Library of Congress, 1988), p. 37.

13. Ibid., p. 40.

14. Ibid., p. 333.

15. Stephen Donadio, et. al., eds., *The New York Public Library Book of 20th Century Quotations* (New York: Warner Books, 1992), p. 126.

Where to Write

Organizations Supporting Official English and Limitations on Immigration

The American Immigration Control Foundation (AICF)
P.O. Box 525
Monterey, VA 24465
Publishes monthly newsletter: *Border Watch*

Americans for Immigration Control (AIC)
717 Second St., NE, Suite 307
Washington, DC 20002

Federation for American Immigration Reform (FAIR)
1666 Connecticut Ave. NW, Suite 400
Washington, DC 20009
Publishes reports including: *Rethinking Immigration Policy* and *Ten Steps to Securing America's Borders*

U.S. English
818 Connecticut Ave. NW, Suite 200
Washington, DC 20006
Publishes newsletter: *Update* ; other publications include *One Nation...Indivisible?*

Organizations Supporting Immigrant and Language Minority Rights

Center for Applied Linguistics (CAL)
1118 22nd Street, NW,
Washington, DC 20037

Center for Immigrants Rights (CIR)
48 Street, Marks Place, Fourth Floor
New York, NY 10003

Multicultural Education, Training, and Advocacy, Inc.
(META)
240A Elm Street, Suite 22
Somerville, MA 02144

National Association for Bilingual Education (NABE)
Union Center Plaza
1220 L Street NW, Suite 605
Washington, DC 20005
Publishes newsletter: *NABE NEWS* and journal: *NABE JOURNAL*

National Council of La Raza (NCLR)
810 First St. NE, Third Floor
Washington, DC 20002
Publications include *Beyond Ellis Island: Hispanics—Immigrants and Americans* and a quarterly newsletter, *Education Network News.*

Glossary

Americanization—The process of adopting the language and customs of the United States while giving up those of one's native country. It is the process of assimilation (see next entry) as applied to the United States.

assimilation—The process of minorities adjusting to the majority or mainstream culture and language: for example, in America, non-English speakers learning English and American customs.

bilingual—Speaking or using two languages.

bilingual education—Teaching students who know little or no English in both their native language and English; bilingual education may or may not include helping students keep and improve their native language while also learning English.

bilingual/bicultural education—Teaching students who know little or no English by using the language and customs of both their native language and English.

English as a second language (ESL)—Teaching non-English speakers reading, writing, and speaking English the way English-speaking Americans are taught Spanish or French, for instance; ESL may or may not include some use of the students' native language.

English language amendment (ELA)—A proposed amendment to the U.S. Constitution that would make English the official language of the country.

immersion—Teaching non-English speakers using English but not the students' native language; immersion may or may not involve special materials and methods to help the students.

language majority—People who speak the main language of a place (in the United States, English speakers are members of the language majority).

language minority—A group not speaking the main language of a place (in the United States, non-English speakers are members of language minorities).

maintenance bilingual education (MBE)—Teaching students English while at the same time helping them keep and improve skills in their native language.

melting pot—The idea of the United States as a place where people with different backgrounds mix together until they lose their differences and all become "Americans."

monolingual—Speaking only one language.

multicultural education—Studying all the different groups that make up American society as part of a student's education.

multilingual—Speaking or using several languages.

nativism—Favoring people already living in the United States over immigrants: often involves trying to limit immigration, supporting English-only laws, and celebrating mainstream or majority American culture.

official English laws—Laws requiring the use of English by government employees when dealing with the public.

Official English movement—The activity of groups that believe all Americans should know and use English; the Official English movement supports, for instance, the use of English by government employees and opposes long-term bilingual and bilingual/bicultural education.

transitional bilingual education (TBE)—Teaching students all their academic subjects (mathematics, reading, science, history, etc.) in their native languages until they learn enough English to attend classes conducted only in English.

two-way or dual language bilingual education—Teaching English to students with another native language, while in the same classroom teaching native-English speakers the foreign language of their classmates.

Further Reading

Books:

Baron, Dennis. *The English-Only Question: An Official Language for Americans?* New Haven, Conn.: Yale University Press, 1990.

Chavez, Linda. *Out of the Barrio: Toward a New Politics of Hispanic Assimilation.* New York: BasicBooks: A Division of HarperCollins Publishers, 1991.

Crawford, James. *Hold Your Tongue: Bilingualism and the Politics of "English-Only."* Reading, Mass.: Addison-Wesley Publishing Company, 1992.

————, ed. *Language Loyalties: A Source Book on the Official English Controversy.* Chicago: The University of Chicago Press, 1992.

Davis, Marilyn P. *Mexican Voices/American Dreams: An Oral History of Mexican Immigration to the United States.* New York: Henry Holt and Company, 1990.

Dudley, William, et. al., eds. *Immigration: Opposing Viewpoints.* San Diego: Greenhaven Press, Inc., 1990.

Harlan, Judith. *Bilingualism in the United States: Conflict and Controversy.* New York: Franklin Watts, 1991.

Hoexter, Corrine K. *From Canton to California: The Epic of Chinese Immigration.* New York: Four Winds Press, 1976.

Lamm, Richard D. and Gary Imhoff. *The Immigration Time Bomb: The Fragmenting of America.* New York: Truman Talley Books/E. P. Dutton, 1985.

Long, Robert Emmet, ed. *Immigration to the United States.* New York: The H. W. Wilson Company, 1992.

Nguyen-Hong-Nhiem, Lucy and Joel Martin, Halpern, eds. *The Far East Comes Near: Autobiographical Accounts of Southeast Asian Students in America.* Amherst, Mass.: The University of Massachusetts Press, 1989.

Padilla, Amado M. et. al., eds. *Bilingual Education: Issues and Strategies.* Newbury Park, Calif.: Sage Publications, 1990.

Porter, Rosalie Pedalino. *Forked Tongue: The Politics of Bilingual Education.* New York: BasicBooks, Inc., 1990.

Rodriguez, Richard. *Hunger of Memory: The Education of Richard Rodriguez.* New York: Bantam Books, 1983.

Santoli, Al. *New Americans, An Oral History: Immigrants and Refugees in the U.S. Today.* New York: Viking, 1988.

Simon, Paul. *The Tongue-Tied American: Confronting the Foreign Language Crisis.* New York: Continuum, 1980.

Topping, Elena, ed., *Ethnic Heritage and Language Schools in America.* Washington, D.C.: Library of Congress, 1988.

Weyr, Thomas. *Hispanic U.S.A.: Breaking the Melting Pot.* New York: Harper & Row Publishers, 1988.

Periodical Articles

McCarthy, Abagail. "A Common Currency: The Gift of a Single Tongue," *Commonwealth,* May 4, 1990.

"No Official Language: A Federal Judge Knocks Down Arizona's English-Only Law." *Time,* February 19, 1990.

"The Balkans, U.S.A." *National Review,* March 5, 1990.

Thernstrom, Abigail M. "Bilingual Miseducation." *Commentary,* February, 1990.

Whitman, David, et al. "For Latinos, a Growing Divide." *U.S. News and World Report,* August 10, 1987.

Newspaper Articles

Clark, Rebecca L. and Jeffrey S. Passel, "Immigrants: A Cost or a Benefit?: Studies are Deceptive." *The New York Times,* September 3, 1993.

Editorial. "Turning Loopy Over Language." *The New York Times,* May 18, 1993.

Huddle, Donald L. "Immigrants: A Cost or a Benefit?: A Growing Burden." *The New York Times*, September 3, 1993.

Kamber, Victor. "Watch Your Language: English Shouldn't Be Official." *The New York Times*, October 22, 1993.

Mydans, Seth. " A New Tide of Immigration Brings Hostility to the Surface, Poll Finds." *The New York Times*, June 27, 1993.

O'Leary, Bradley S. "Watch Your Language: English Should Be Official." *The New York Times*, October 22, 1993.

Sontag, Deborah. "English as a Precious Language: Immigrants Hungry for Literacy Find That Classes Are Few." *The New York Times*, August 29, 1993.

————. "A Fervent 'No' to Assimilation in New America." *The New York Times*, June 29, 1993.

————. "New Immigrants Test Nation's Heartland." *The New York Times*, October 18, 1993.

Weiner, Tim. "On These Shores Immigrants Find a New Wave of Hostility." *The New York Times*, June 13, 1993.

Index

O

"Official English", 6, 16, 20, 29
"Official English Amendment", 18
Out of the Barrio, 12-13
Oregon, 57
Orthodox Jews, 68

P

Pachon, Harry, 78
Pennsylvania, 28-29
Pennsylvania Railroad, 31
pocho, 43
Porter, Rosalie Pedalino, 70, 92
Pratt, Larry, 55
"Proposition 63", 55
Protestant, 30
Puerto Ricans, 49

R

Rea, Samuel, 31
Reagan, Ronald, 10, 54, 62
recent arrivals, 5, 6
Rodriguez, Richard, 21, 41-43, 49-50
Ronstadt, Linda, 83
Ros, Chanthouk, 45, 50
Rosenblatt, Judge Paul, 57
Russians, 39

S

San Antonio, Texas, 7
San Francisco, California, 19, 46, 61, 63
San Quentin, 77
Saturday schools, 92-93
segregation, 10
Sesame Street, 83
Shorris, Earl, 77
Simon, Senator Paul, 90, 92
slaves, 28
Smith, William, 29

Spanish-American League Against Discrimination (SALAD), 56
Switzerland, 89

T

Tampa Tribune, 75
Tanton, John, 11-12, 53-54
Tellez, Madelin, 45
Tennessee, 54
Texas, 30
Tower of Babel, 15-16
Transitional Bilingual Education (TBE), 65
Two-way bilingual education, 65
(*See also*: Dual language bilingual education)

U

Uprooted, The, 95
"U.S. English", 6, 11, 12, 16, 18, 19-20, 54
U.S. News and World Report, 78

V

Vietnam, 9
Vietnam War, 52
Vietnamese Americans, 47
Virginia, 55
Voting Rights Act, 84, 85

W

Washington, 57
Wattenberg, Ben J., 79
Weil, Frank A., 89
Weyr, Thomas, 59
World War I, 33, 34, 36

Y

Yiddish, 68
Yniguez, Maria-Kelly, 57
Yup'ik, 61

DATE DUE			